THE
GUIDED
MEDITATION
HANDBOOK

ALSO BY MAX HIGHSTEIN

BOOK
THE HEALING WATERFALL
100 Guided Imagery scripts for Counselors, Healers, & Clergy

GUIDED IMAGERY AUDIO PROGRAMS
Most of the scripts included in this book and more can be obtained as beautifully recorded audio programs at TheHealingWaterfall.com, and elsewhere online. **Some of the most popular include:**

- The Healing Waterfall
- Morning Meditation
- Sleep Well Tonight
- Visiting Mother Mary
- Good Boundaries
- Self Esteem
- Saying Goodbye (Grief and Loss)
- Guided Imagery for PTSD
- Sanctuary of Peace
- Meet Your Guardian Angel
- 12-Step Guided Meditations

ONLINE COURSES
- Intuition Retreat: Develop Your Intuitive & Psychic Ability
- Heart Meditations
- Master The Art Of Deep Listening
- Awaken To Miracles With Padre Pio
- Opening Doors For The Spiritual Creative
- Releasing Fear: Say Goodbye to Anxiety
- Say Goodbye To Anger
- Attracting A Great Relationship
- 12-Step Guided Meditations
- Car Peace: Make Your Car A Stress-Free Sanctuary

MUSIC ALBUMS

- Flying Not Falling
- Flight Plans
- Touch The Sky
- Stars
- Path Of The Heart
- Intuition: Music To Guide You Deeper
- Daydreams
- Sacred Journeys
- Healing Journey
- Gentle Music for Massage

SESSIONS AND SERVICES

Max Highstein offers intuitive counseling sessions, custom made guided imagery recordings, and custom music composing.

Visit TheHealingWaterfall.com, MaxHighstein.com, and MaxHighsteinMusic.com for information about all of Max Highstein's work.

THE GUIDED MEDITATION HANDBOOK

THE COMPLETE GUIDE TO WRITING, LEADING, & RECORDING GUIDED MEDITATIONS

MAX HIGHSTEIN

GRATITUDE
& APPRECIATION

This book was made possible by the many people who have supported me and my work over the years:

All who have purchased and enjoyed my guided imagery and my music, and especially those who have taken the time to write to me with thoughtful notes of appreciation.

Jim Moeller, who has helped bring my guided imagery to the world though his persistant marketing efforts over the long haul.

Those who have so generously supported my work financially.

The many gifted teachers and healers who have opened my mind and enlightened my heart.

All those who came before me in my field, helping to lead the way.

My parents, who provided an atmosphere of creativity and freedom to explore, and my brothers who set such inspiring examples of what might be possible.

With extra special thanks, gratitude, appreciation and love as always, to my wife and forever friend, Michele.

Max Highstein, August, 2019

CONTENTS

INTRODUCTION

FIRST CONTACT

The first guided meditation I ever experienced was in a therapy session decades ago. The therapist had me lie back in a recliner, and close my eyes. Then she said, "Now Max, become aware of your toes…" And the way she pronounced the word "toes" sounded so silly to me that I burst out laughing.

But to be honest, I think it was my discomfort in the situation that produced my laughter. Looking back on it, I must have felt self-conscious. And I suspect I wasn't prepared to let this person, who I wasn't sure I trusted, tell me what to do while I was lying down in front of her with my eyes closed. In a nutshell, I felt too vulnerable, and my laughter was a shield.

Nevertheless, she continued the process, gradually working our way up from my toes until we got to the top of my head. Then she asked me to walk through a door into a room on the left side of my head and see what was there. I didn't see much in that room, and told her so. And then she asked me to walk through a door into a room on the right side of my head.

Suddenly my head filled with a bright light and I found myself crying uncontrollably.

Depending on your philosophical orientation, you may suppose that I either experienced a sudden and dramatic release of pent-up tension, was visited by a spiritual force, or came into contact with my own higher consciousness. From my vantage point all these years later I'd say it was all of the above. But at the time, all I knew was that something profound had happened, and that I felt much better than I had before we started.

Such was my introduction to our subject at hand.

GUIDED IMAGERY & GUIDED MEDITATION

At the time, the work my therapist had done was and still is referred to as "guided imagery." You could also say that she led me on "a guided meditation." The two phrases are closely related, and in many ways interchangeable.

In guided imagery, one person guides another to imagine (image-in) something, thereby leading the listener into a meditative state.

This is a book about using guided imagery to develop, perform, or produce your own guided meditation programs or sessions. This material comes from my experience developing and publishing well over 100 guided meditation programs, as well as leading count-less spontaneous live guided imagery sessions with individuals and groups, all over the course of the past 35 years.

SOME BACKGROUND

Although I was formally trained in counseling, (my BA was in music, my graduate work in psychology) my initial knowledge of guided imagery and guided meditation was gained through absorption. I learned about it by attending a multitude of programs, courses, and programs related to personal growth, healing, and spirituality, all as a consumer. The rest I learned by doing, noticing the results, and refining my approach accordingly.

For the several first guided meditations I produced, I wrote the scripts, hired professional voice actors, recorded them in commercial recording studios, and then composed the music backgrounds, scoring music to the narration. Eventually, I learned how to voice the scripts myself in a way that I felt met the standard established by the wonderful actors I had first hired. Along the way I also acquired my own recording studio, which was convenient considering how much of this work I would eventually do.

At first I did all of the production, packaging, marketing, and promotion of my guided meditation programs. Mine were some of the very first programs of their kind to reach a wide audience in bookstores, and they made quite an impact, helping to launch this new category. But soon I turned the marketing over a record company that also began handling my music albums.

Years later, with the digital age in full bloom, I came to once again oversee most my own publishing. Today my guided meditation and music catalog is widely available on most all the current digital platforms. In addition, some of my guided imagery work is also part of a series of online courses I have authored over the years, also available online.

YOUR MOVE
Today, multitudes of guided meditations are virtually everywhere, and although you may not have the advantage of "getting in on it early," as I did, you can produce and publish your own programs alongside mine in all of those same platforms. It's a field open to everyone, so I encourage you to wade in and enjoy the process. The fact that you are reading this indicates that you care about the quality of the work you would like to put out into the world, and want to make it your best. I appreciate that a great deal, and I hope the information and guidance in this book will be helpful to you.

And so, to begin: *Become aware of your toes...*

CHAPTER 1

WRITING YOUR SCRIPT

Whether you plan to write a formal script for a guided meditation that you will record word-for-word, or are interested in leading spontaneous live meditations, this chapter will provide an overview of the elements of an effective program.

There are lots of different kinds of guided meditations for different purposes, but most of them have a few basic things in common. At the heart of things, your program will most likely include:

- An Induction, usually covered in the first few sentences

- An optional Transition, leading the listener toward the main body of the program

- The main body of your program

- An "Outro" or ending.

Let's take a look at these different parts in detail, using some examples.

INTRODUCING THE INDUCTION

An effective guided meditation will help your listener shift their attention from their normal waking state of consciousness to a more relaxed and receptive mode: Not fully awake, not quite asleep, but a kind of daydreamy space in between. Once there, your guided meditation may be about working on emotional issues, visualizing success, accessing higher awareness, or just enjoying a period of peaceful relaxation. Regardless of the goal of your guided meditation, to achieve that shift into relaxation you'll typically be starting with something called an *induction*.

This part of your guided meditation should be designed to *induce* a relaxed state, and that's why we call it an induction. Here's an example of an induction I've used on many, many guided meditations:

Make yourself comfortable, and close your eyes. [short pause]

Take a slow deep breath, and let go of any tension, as you feel yourself sinking into the surface you're resting on, becoming still more comfortable and relaxed. [short pause]

Take another slow, deep breath, and release your thoughts, letting them drift far away. [short pause]

And take another slow, deep breath, and know that in this moment, all is well. [short pause]

There is actually quite a bit of guided meditation technology packed into these few sentences. Here are a few things to note:

I've used the words, *comfortable, relaxed, slow, deep, drift, resting*. All of these words contribute to the listener's sense that they are safe and secure, so they can open to receive the input that follows. It's not uncommon to also repeat some of these words, especially "relaxed" and "comfortable," at various points in the program.

I've invited the listener to take several slow deep breaths. This accomplishes a few things. First, it sets up an expectation that we are doing something special, because really, when in our normal daily activities do take slow, deep breaths? We're doing something a little different today, and this first step helps to set it apart from the ordinary, right at the outset.

But beyond that, deep breaths are helpful from a more physical perspective. Taking conscious deep breaths brings our focus to our body, helps us become aware of tension, and helps us let it go. When we take a few deep breaths, we begin to feel better almost immediately, and the meditation has only just begun. Never underestimate the power of a few slow, deep breaths!

There are three breaths, and three is a magic number in this case, because it's high enough to be a series, with a beginning, middle and end. By the third breath my listener has already completed something, and whether or not they are aware of it, that brings a subtle sense of satisfaction and accomplishment. Already, my listener and I have succeeded together, and she's even more ready to go along with me on an inner journey. Never underestimate the power of the number "three!"

But wait, there's more! I've said "sinking into the surface you're resting on." If I were in the same room as my listener, and could see what they were sitting on, I might have said "chair." But since this induction was used on a recording, for all I know they may be sitting on a car seat or a log. The point is, we always want to avoid saying anything the listener might disagree with. If I say "chair," and they're sitting on a couch, the difference might be enough to bring them back to their busy intellect—the same place we're trying to give them a break from.

Also, I happen to like "sinking into the surface you're resting on" because it has the nice alliteration of "sinking" and "surface," and it includes the word "resting." You may have another way of inviting your listener to settle in, but the takeaway here is that your words are important, so give thought to what you say, and choose them carefully.

Here are a few other things you might say in an induction:

- It's time to set aside all your cares and worries

- Bring your focus into the here and now

- Settle into the relaxing sound of the music.

- Breathe in light, and breathe out love

- Let the sound of the music (my voice, this bell, the ocean waves, etc.) carry you deeper within

- Surround yourself with light, and feel a sense of peace begin to wash over you

MAKING A TRANSITION

Deep breaths or otherwise, your induction will help your listener become comfortable and relaxed, and set them up for what's to come. The next part of your script can build on that relaxation base, and help your listener shift further away from their normal world, and into something beyond. Let's call this part of your program the *transition* or *transitional phase*. Here are examples of some ideas you might use for your transitional phase.

- Ascending or descending a stairway, step by step

- Floating up through the ceiling to another dimension

- Drifting inside a bubble of light

- Walking through a doorway into another world

- Stepping onto a train, boat, plane, car, horse, giant turtle, etc.

All of these examples use the idea of going somewhere apart from the our normal setting. Depending upon the main focus of your program, your transition may relate more to the physical world, as in a stairway or train, or the spiritual or metaphysical, as in a bubble of light.

If I'm writing a program that's oriented toward working through emotional issues I might use the idea of *descending* a stairway, since that can be a metaphor for going deeper into the subconscious mind.

Here's an excerpt from my program, Good Boundaries, using the descending stairway idea:

> Open the door. Before you are five stairs down to a landing, and you can see a soft light coming from the other side of the landing, at the bottom of the stairs.
>
> As you step down onto the first step, take a moment to consider the following question: *What do I do for others that should be their responsibility to do themselves?* [30 second pause]
>
> As you step down to the second step, take a moment to consider this question: *In what situations do I give away my time, energy, money, to gain acceptance, love or appreciation?* [30 second pause]
>
> As you step down to the third step, consider this question: *In what ways do I leave my own center and ignore my own truth to try and get my physical or emotional needs met?* [30 second pause]

And so on.

In the example above, I used each stair as a way of introducing ideas I wanted the listener to begin considering. This is a convenient way of getting them ready for the next stage of the program. As you can see, there is quite a bit of heady stuff packed into this transition. If this were a simple relaxation program, that would be way too much serious content. But here it's appropriate, because the program is specifically oriented toward helping the listener solve a particular problem.

In order to make this part of the program more digestible, I voiced the recording slowly (as I normally do), and included nice long pauses between each step. Gentle background music helps tie things together.

Here's a transition example from my program, Visiting Angels. This one uses the idea of *ascending* a stairway, combined with the color spectrum:

> Imagine you're walking up a wide flight of stairs, toward a higher level of awareness. And as you walk, notice that the steps beneath your feet are a brilliant red color. This ruby red color seems to flow right up through you, bringing a burst of pure energy, to start you on your journey. [30 second pause]
>
> Walking higher, you see that the steps have now changed to orange. The orange color flows through you, and gives you strength and support, to sustain you throughout your journey. [30 second pause]
>
> Moving higher, the steps have become bright yellow. Now this yellow color flows up into you, clearing your mind, and preparing you for new insight and discovery. [30 second pause]
>
> As you continue farther, the stairs change to a deep emerald green. The color green gently enfolds you, bringing comfort and balance. [30 second pause]
>
> Climbing still higher, the stairs have changed to a beautiful blue. Now this blue color lightly encircles you, bringing a soothing sense of serenity. [30 second pause]

And so on.

Since the subject of this program is spiritual, I used the ascending stairway and rising hues as a way of helping the listener tap into higher awareness. The rising color spectrum also happens to correspond with the chakras or energy centers in the body, beginning with red at the base of the spine. I also packed in a bit of motivational content with each color, suggesting energy, strength, balance, and so on. Incidentally, Visiting Angels was written about 20 years before Good Boundaries, but as you can see, my approach has been fairly consistent.

QUICKER TRANSITIONS

For some guided meditations you may want to skip a long transition, and get to the main theme of your program more quickly. Here are a few examples of a more streamlined transition.

Waking From A Dream

Here's a transition excerpted from 12-Step Guided Meditations, a series of guided meditations for 12-Step recovery programs. This one leads the listener to "wake up" in new surroundings.

> Imagine you've been sleeping a deep, sound sleep for many hours, and you're just beginning to stir awake. And the first thing you notice is that you're waking up on a soft bed of pine needles, on the ground, surrounded by ancient fir trees. It's just before dawn, and the air is quite cool, the light is dim, and there's a foggy mist in the air. You can smell the scent of pine, and the damp coolness of the earth. It's quiet, and any sound is blanketed by the mist. Everything is a palette of soft greens, browns, and grays. Standing up, you begin to walk along a path through the trees, and you can feel the spongy ground beneath your feet.

Notice the use of tactile sense (soft bed of pine needles, and cool, misty air), then sight (fir trees, dim light), then smell (the scent of pine), and then sound. Then it comes back to the tactile sense again with the spongy ground. So in this example, while we ask the listener to make a quick transition to a new space, we help by immediately filling in lots of information about where they are, helping them to experience a sense of place.

There's a much easier way to do this of course. You could simply say something like, "Imagine you're in your favorite place. Perhaps it's a beach, or the woods, or a mountain meadow. Pick a place that's just right for you."

You could do that, but I generally prefer not to. Your listeners may not have a vivid imagination, or be quick enough to come up with a scene that is as immersive as something you could describe in detail. Unless you know that your audience has done lots of guided imagery and are great visualizers, it's usually best to put in the work, fill in details for them, and help place them in a world they can enjoy. (I've made an exception to this rule in the program, Saying Goodbye, which I'll describe in detail in the following chapter.)

Walking Through A Doorway

This transition is from Visiting Padre Pio, a program introducing the listener to a spiritual master. It first brings them into their spiritual heart, and then leads them through a doorway.

> Bring your awareness into your spiritual heart, in the center of your chest, and notice a softness there, a feeling of peace. Take a moment to enjoy this feeling, as you quietly focus in your heart, and follow your breath, in, and out. [20 second pause.]
>
> Bring yourself more fully into your heart, as if you were standing there now, inside a cozy room. Soon, you'll notice a doorway, and as you walk through it, you'll find yourself transported to a lovely garden, on the grounds of an ancient monastery. The garden is a rustic one, with flower beds, shrubs, and olive and fig trees, all lovingly cared for. The plants and trees seem to glow with a heavenly light, their colors soft, and radiant. The bird songs here are sweet, and musical. And the air is filled with a delicate scent of roses, lilacs, and other flowers, all fresh from a recent rain shower.

Again you can spot the use of sight, sound, smell, and tactile sense from the recent rain.

Just Be There

Here is a transition from Sleep Well Tonight, a guided meditation for sleep. In this example, we simply ask the listener to imagine they are "there," aided by the use of lots of imagery. What you can't tell from reading, is that this program uses the sound of ocean waves in the background to greatly enhance the sense of place. Another program in this sleep series uses the sound of an overnight train moving along the tracks; and in another there is the sound of a mountain stream.

Imagine you're standing on the shore of a lovely tropical island. It's evening and the sun is just now setting, and you watch as the orange ball begins to touch the horizon, casting a beautiful golden glow over the sea. The light blue sky is beginning to turn yellow and pink where it meets the ocean, deepening into shades of dark blue and purple, higher up.

Perhaps a surfer is taking his last ride of the day, and a sentry of pelicans glides softly across the placid scene, heading for a place to rest for the night. Earth is ready to welcome the nighttime, and the sky has begun to draw its curtain on another day.

In all of the examples listed above, the transition phase helps the listener make a shift from their normal state of consciousness to a deeper feeling of relaxation. Using descriptive imagery and cues about touch, feeling, and in some cases smell, the transition brings them into a setting far removed from their normal physical reality. I encourage you to get creative in your transitions, and make your writing rich and juicy. Don't be afraid to go overboard here. You can always edit and bring it back into line before you're finished.

THE MAIN BODY OF YOUR PROGRAM

Now we come to the heart of your guided meditation, the main body of your program.

In the simplest form, a guided meditation can be about helping your listener take a quiet break from their day and relax. Technically, I could say to you, "Close your eyes and imagine you're floating on a cloud," hum a few bars of Pachelbel's Canon in D, and call that a guided meditation.

But there are so many other things you can do with guided meditation, beyond simple relaxation. A partial list follows.

Health

- Sleep
- Pain management
- Stress relief
- Weight & body image
- Surgery prep
- Mind-Body connection

Personal Growth

- Develop healthy boundaries
- Release stored fear, anger, sadness
- Reprogram negative habits like jealousy, judgment, hatred
- Develop empathy and compassion
- Build self esteem

Worldly Success

- Increase prosperity
- Find a better job
- Improve performance in work, sports, etc.
- Find a relationship

Creativity

- Spark imagination
- Improve work habits
- Tap into new ideas
- Consider difficult problems from all sides
- Stimulate expression

Spiritual Topics

- Explore a past life
- Connect to spirit guides, angels, and departed souls
- Look into possible future scenarios
- Experience a variety of pure meditation techniques

As you can see, the main body of your program might be about drifting along to simply relax, or helping your listener to get some deeper work done. In the next chapter we'll look at complete scripts from many different kinds of programs, to help fill in more of the picture of what guided meditations can do.

THE "OUTRO" OR ENDING

Let's say you've taken your listener on a lovely inner journey, they've become very relaxed, and perhaps they've even done some deep inner work and learned something new about themselves. Now it's time to bring them back to their full waking state of consciousness, so they don't walk away bumping into things. You could just take a page from hypnotism and say, "and when I snap my fingers, you'll be wide awake." But that seems kind of rude, doesn't it?

I tend to favor a softer approach. And just as I tend to begin all of my guided meditation programs with a similar induction, I also like to end my programs in a similar way. Here's the ending I typically use:

> It will soon be time to bring this journey to a close. But first, take a moment to thank yourself forgiving yourself this gift.
>
> Bring your awareness gently back to your physical surroundings. Take your time, and when you're ready, open your eyes, and feel awake, alert, and refreshed.

You'll notice that I began by saying "It will soon be time..." I'm not saying, "OK, times up!" I'm letting the listener know that we're getting ready to wrap things up, slowly easing them out of their relaxation.

Then I ask them to start being aware of their outside world. You could also say, "become aware of your body," or "begin to notice yourself back in your room."

And I love ending with the phrase, "and when you're ready, open your eyes, and feel awake, alert, and refreshed." It's nice to send the listener on their way on a high note.

Right about now I bet you're thinking you caught a typo in the second sentence. Nope! I intend to say "forgiving yourself this gift," rather than "for giving yourself this gift." It is admittedly hard to tell the difference when read aloud. But I enjoy the notion of slipping in a vote for self-forgiveness when I can. Most of us can use more of it.

A WORD ABOUT AFFIRMATIONS

Some guided meditations include affirmations, or short statements that claim something positive for the listener. Affirmations can be helpful, or not, depending upon the way they are used.

In the early days of the personal growth movement, you might have seen people saying or writing a specific affirmation over and over. It was sort of like a bad student writing "I won't talk in class" on the blackboard 100 times.

Unfortunately, that process doesn't do much for us. Why not? Because the repeated message doesn't go any deeper than the intellect, and the intellect isn't where change happens. Changing a behavior or lifestyle pattern has to come from deep within, and simply repeating a sentence over and over again doesn't get down there.

The way I suggest using affirmations is to repeat them a few times inwardly, listen deeply, and let them bounce around inside. Chances are, they're going to bump into some contradictory messages. For example, if you say "I am open to wealth and prosperity on all levels," and let that message in deep, it might run into an inner script that says something like, "I don't deserve more money than I already have." That collision is a good thing, because it brings the negative script into our awareness. If a negative one is in there, we need to know about it and bring it up to the surface so we can release it.

So I suggest using affirmations like a kind of "depth charge," to go down deep and clear out the sludge. And in my guided meditation scripts, I frame them this way:

> Listen to the following affirmations, and allow them find their way deep within you.

I also use a technique in mixing the recording where I repeat each affirmation two or three times, each time softer than before, and add a little reverb (see Recording Your Program, "A Bit Of Verb.") That helps the listener get the sense of going deeper.

When it comes to writing the affirmations themselves, wording is a delicate art. You'll want to always frame them in a positive way. For example:

"I'm not letting obstacles stop me from achieving my goal"

could be improved by saying:

"I overcome all obstacles to achieve my goal."

You'll also want to frame your affirmations in the present tense:

"I will be healthy and strong"

becomes:

"I am healthy and strong."

And try to keep affirmations short. Think of them like advertising, poetry, or song lyrics. The fewer words that can be used, the more powerful they can be.

EDITING YOUR SCRIPT

I mentioned earlier how important choosing your words can be. Let's look a little further into this now. Say you've written out a draft of your guided meditation, and have the basic components in place. Now it's time to begin polishing your work. Read over every line out loud, and listen for the following:

Any language that is stuffy, or academic sounding. Keep the writing conversational and informal. This is not the time to impress your listener with big words. It's not a school paper, it's a guided meditation. If you can say something more simply, say it more simply.

Use contractions wherever they sound right. Instead of saying, "It is time to relax," say "It's time to relax." The words will roll off your tongue more easily that way, and you'll be more pleasant to listen to. "Imagine you are walking down a quiet path" becomes "Imagine you're walking down a quiet path."

Use adjectives and adverbs to juice up your imagery. Why say "Imagine you're walking along a path through a meadow," when you could say "Imagine you're walking quietly along a winding path, through a lush mountain meadow"? And while you're at it, go ahead and take a few sentences to describe the grass, flowers, and clouds in the sky. Help your listener paint a rich picture in their mind's eye.

GETTING TOUCHY AND SMELLY

While you're painting pictures with words, include the other senses as well. If you're doing a beach meditation, talk about the sound of the waves and sea birds, the smell of the ocean, the feeling of the salt air on the skin, or the feeling of walking on wet sand.

"From the park you hear the happy sound of a carousel. You can almost taste the hotdogs and French fries they sell."
Under the Boardwalk, by Arthur Resnick and Kenny Young.
Rich imagery, as sung by The Drifters.

CHAPTER 2

SCRIPT EXAMPLES
& ANALYSIS

Now we'll look at some complete scripts, consider how they were written, and zero in on what makes them effective.

A SIMPLE RELAXATION PROGRAM: RELAX ON A TROPICAL BEACH

Our first example is a fairly basic relaxation script. You'll find that this one includes many of the same basic elements as the scripts to follow.

> Make yourself comfortable, and close your eyes. Take a slow deep breath, and let go of any tension, as you feel yourself sinking into the surface you're resting on, becoming still more comfortable and relaxed. Take another slow, deep breath, and release your thoughts, letting them drift far away. And take another slow, deep breath, and know that in this moment, all is well.

There's our induction, as described in detail in the previous chapter. The meditation continues...

> Imagine you're taking a walk along a tropical beach, on a summer day. You're on vacation, and you have all the time in the world. And today, you have the beach all to yourself. The weather is perfect, and as you walk along, you can smell the salt air, and feel the light ocean mist on your face. Perhaps you're walking barefoot, on the packed sand just by the water's edge. And as you walk, you can feel your heels pushing into the sand a little with each step. And now and then the warm water just barely laps up to kiss your feet.

In this program we've skipped using a transition, and jumped right into the main setting, a tropical beach. First we set up the idea that the conditions are great for relaxation: *You've got all the time you need, and the weather is perfect.* Then we introduced content relating to touch and smell: The salt air, the packed sand, and the water on your feet.

You may have noticed that I started three of the sentences in the script above with the word "and." If this were meant to be read as text, that would be a poor choice. But this material is meant to be read aloud in a fairly slow cadence. Here the "ands" help connect the thoughts for the listener. When writing your own script, always read aloud and listen, and adjust your work as needed to insure the best flow.

Sandpipers dart here and there, at the edge of the water. And out beyond the breakers, a small flock of pelicans soar just above the water. Take a moment to simply walk along, take in the scenery and the sounds, and enjoy.

Here we've filled in some of the visual imagery, with the seabirds moving along the sand, and out beyond the waves. Whenever I include the words, "take a moment" as I did above, I pause the narration for a longer period of time, from 20 seconds to a minute, depending on the content, to allow the listener to visualize and integrate the imagery.

Soon you come to an inviting lounge chair that's been set up for you on the sand, and decide this would be a good time to take a rest. So you settle down and get comfortable, shading your eyes with a nice big straw hat. Now you're completely content to simply lie back, relax, and listen to the sound of the waves.

And here we've included the sense of hearing, with the sound of the waves. In a guided meditation about the seashore it helps a lot to include a background track of ocean waves, as I did in this program. Find an audio track that has gentle, even wave sounds, and be sure to mix it far enough in the background that it doesn't overpower the narration.

Your body is loving this restful feeling, and a wonderful wave of deep relaxation begins to gradually make its way all through you. The relaxation moves through your body easily, beginning with your toes, moving up through your feet, and ankles, and into your calves and your knees.

And it makes its way up into your upper legs and hips. Now your legs and hips are completely comfortable, and deeply relaxed. And this wave of peaceful relaxation moves on into your abdomen, and lower back, and your chest and upper back, and they're also feeling completely comfortable, and deeply relaxed.

And this wave of peaceful relaxation flows up into your shoulders, and down your arms, into your hands, and out your fingertips. You're feeling wonderfully calm, and settled.

And so this wave of peaceful energy flows up through your neck, throughout your head, and face, and right out the top of your head. Now your whole body is as relaxed, comfortable, and peaceful as it can be.

A full head-to-toe (or toe-to-head) body relaxation is often included in guided meditations. The writing for this segment tends to be repetitive by nature. So the challenge is to work in at least some variation in the sentences, while keeping a rhythm going. I've repeated the words, "relaxation," and "relaxed," often, because that's the intent, and repetition can help lull the listener into that state. I also don't mind repeating "And" at the beginning of each sentence. That works fine in this context, and helps to tie the body relaxation steps together. When it comes time to record the narration, timing the pauses in body relaxation sequences is especially important. (See Voicing Your Program)

As you listen to the gentle rhythm of the waves, begin to notice the rhythm of your breath. It's a lot like the ocean, wave after wave, peaceful breath after breath.

Begin to follow your breath a little more closely now, and between each breath, pause just for a moment, to enjoy the feeling. Breathe in, pause just a bit, breathe out, pause just a bit—the perfect timing that's comfortable for you. This little pause helps you to really savor each breath. Notice how good each breath feels, and how it nourishes you.

Focusing on the breath and slowing down one's breathing are extremely helpful in fostering any kind of relaxation.

Your body loves this peaceful, relaxing rhythm, like the ocean loves the waves, so perfectly natural, and satisfying. To enjoy this feeling even more, with each breath in, inwardly say the word, "deep," and with each breath out, inwardly say the word, "peace." If that feels good to you, repeat this for some time, as you lie on the beach, on this beautiful summer day, and enjoy the peaceful, relaxing comfort. Stay as long as you like.

This particular program does not include a specific verbal ending.

The narration ends as above, but the program continues beyond the narration for some time with the sound of the ocean waves.

A PAIN MANAGEMENT PROGRAM: RELEASING PAIN

Guided imagery has been used to help manage pain for decades. This program uses relaxation, a staircase transition, color, and awareness techniques to help the listener gain a sense of control over their pain.

Make yourself comfortable, and close your eyes. Take a slow deep breath, and let go of any tension, as you feel yourself sinking into the surface you're resting on, becoming still more comfortable and relaxed. Take another slow, deep breath, and release your thoughts, letting them drift far away. And take another slow, deep breath, and know that in this moment, all is well.

Imagine that within you is a control room: A place free of distractions, and filled with healing energy, where you can easily focus your thoughts, and influence your body's responses very efficiently, and effectively. And imagine you're about to walk up a flight of stairs, toward your control room.

We take the approach of walking up a flight of stairs here, as opposed to walking down. Why? Because in this case we'd like to help the listener to stretch up and out of their body, away from where their pain would tend to be localized, rather than down into it.

The first step is a brilliant ruby red color, and as you step upon it you feel yourself flooded with powerful, bright energies, bringing you a burst a strength to propel you forward.

Your second step is orange, and as the orange color flows through your body it helps you feel grounded and safe, with strong, sustaining support.

The third step is bright yellow, and as you step upon it, you become filled with joy and optimism, a sense that anything is possible, and you can succeed at whatever you put your mind to.

The fourth step is emerald green, and as you step upon it you're filled with a feeling of deep peace, balance, and an inner knowing that all is unfolding perfectly, just as it should.

The sixth step is a clear, bright blue, and as it flows through you it brings mental clarity and focus, and the feeling that you can know whatever you need to know.

Nearing the top of the staircase, you step upon the seventh step, a rich amethyst purple. As you become flooded with this color you can feel your higher mind open, and sense your connection with all the positive forces of the universe, and beyond.

All of these "color steps" include motivational messages that do several things. They offer the listener a sense of control and optimism, suggest that all is well, and help set up the notion that they can promote change using their mind. The mind-body connection in regard to pain and illness is well documented by science.

Stepping forward onto the landing, you'll find yourself in a beautiful, dome shaped room, filled with golden white light, and delicate soft energy that seems to envelope and embrace you. This is your control room, a space designed to help you connect with all that is good, and create deep and lasting positive changes within you. The work you're about to do here will help you move through the world with more ease and comfort, and enjoy your life more fully.

There's a comfortable chair in your control room, and you know that you've got a lot to do today, so you take a seat.

To begin, do a quick inner scan of your body, and notice the part that's highlighting, for you to release pain. That's where you'll be focusing today.

Imagine that the pain you experience wants to better reveal its identity to you, and is beginning to take on its own three dimensional appearance. Notice or imagine its size and shape. Imagine its color. Imagine the texture of its surface. If you were to touch this, would it feel solid, squishy, spongy, crinkly, or another way? And if it were to make a sound, what would it sound like?

Here the listener has the opportunity to objectify their pain, and begin to gain a sense of direct control over it.

> We can assume that your pain exists for a reason, but the reason might not be what you think it is. Although it may be connected to something going on physically in your body, it might also be connected to something going on mentally, emotionally, in relationship to other people, or about some other aspect of your life.

> First, ask your pain what it's been trying to tell you about your physical body, perhaps about something you've been doing or not doing, eating or not eating, and so on. Take a moment to listen carefully to what your pain has to say.

> Now ask your pain what it's been trying to tell you about your feelings and emotions, and if anything's been bothering you that you might need to clear up.

> Ask your pain if there's anything else it's been trying to tell you, that it thinks you need to know.

> Now, ask your pain what you might need to do or change, in order for it to not need to get your attention so much. Take some time to receive this important information, and be very clear about any steps you'll be taking to make a change.

One of the valuable things guided meditation can offer us is the opportunity for deeper insight. When we are in a relaxed state of mind, and our imagination has been stimulated, we can reach beyond our normal everyday intellect. We're able to bring in intuitive awareness, and information from our unconscious mind, that we normally don't have access to. Using the idea of asking our pain to talk to us about itself, as in the questions above, provides an opening for new insight and information, and allows us to highlight what we may already know, but have not been paying attention to.

> Imagine you're taking all the information you've just received, and placing it on one sheet of paper, entitled, *Information From My Pain*. Now imagine you're rolling that paper up, and placing it in a chute in the wall of your control room. There is a button next to the chute. Once you press that button, the paper, with all

the information on it, will be sent up the chute, and filed away in your system, so you can access it again whenever you need to. Press the button now. The paper flies up the chute with a whoosh, and the information has been filed.

This device prevents the listener from feeling she has to break out of the meditation and write everything down. We're betting that any information of importance will be remembered, and that it's more crucial to stay in meditation till the end of the program.

You've now received all the information your pain had to give you, filed it away, and are prepared to make any changes you need to make. So, your pain won't be needed nearly as much from now on. It's time to clear it out of your body, now.

Imagine that the clear, golden white light from your control room is beginning to shine on your pain. Soon it begins to change color, and take on that golden white hue, and before long, it begins to shrink, growing smaller and smaller. Take some time to watch, as the golden white light continues to shine on your pain, until it's so small you can hardly see it.

Now a gentle, rainbow colored healing rain begins to fall on the area where your pain has been, dissolving and washing away any residue. Take some time to experience this gentle, healing rain as it clears and releases any remaining pain from your body, now.

The above two paragraphs are the heart of this guided meditation, the main reason the listener signed on. We take long pauses after each paragraph with background music but no narration, to give the listener plenty of time to absorb the idea and make it work for them. Looking back over this part of the program, I notice that it's something that could have been expanded upon in more detail. One could elaborate on the pain taking in the golden white light, and how and why that makes it shrink. In the second paragraph, there could be additional information about the body receiving the healing rain, opening up each cell individually getting what it needs, and so on.

From now on, any time you begin to experience pain, simply take a moment to listen to any message your pain may have for you, and then imagine that gentle, rainbow colored healing rain dissolving, clearing, and releasing the pain from your body.

It will soon be time to bring this journey to a close. But first, ask for a sphere of light to be placed all around you, and this experience, so that all the positive benefits will stay with you, and anything that you've released can be left behind. Take a moment to thank yourself forgiving yourself this gift.

Bring your awareness gently back to your physical surroundings. Take your time, and when you're ready, open your eyes, and feel awake, alert, and refreshed.

A GUIDED SLEEP MEDITATION: SLEEP WELL TONIGHT

The first paragraph changes our standard induction a bit to suit the theme of this bedtime guided meditation.

Make yourself comfortable, in your favorite position for falling asleep, and close your eyes. Take a slow, full deep breath, and let it go. It's time to set the world aside, let go of your day, and begin your gentle transition into sleep. And take another slow, full, deep breath, and breathe out any tension in your body. All there is to do now is relax, rest, and be restored.

Imagine you're standing on the shore of a lovely tropical island. It's evening and the sun is just now setting, and you watch as the orange ball begins to touch the horizon, casting a beautiful golden glow over the sea. The light blue sky is beginning to glow yellow and pink where it meets the ocean, deepening into shades of dark blue and purple, higher up.

Perhaps a surfer is taking his last ride of the day, and a sentry of pelicans glides softly across the placid scene, heading for a place to rest for the night. Earth is ready to welcome the nighttime, and the sky has begun to draw its curtain on another day.

There is no "transition" phase in this guided meditation. I assume the listener wants to go to sleep and is ready to jump in. But there is lots of nice imagery to help establish the sense of place.

Your favorite spot, a little ways down the beach, is a little hide-away cottage with a screened-in porch, where you can lie on a comfy bed, listen to the waves, and let the sounds rock you gently to sleep, and so you begin your walk home. Barefoot at the edge of the warm, tropical water, you love the way your heels sink in a little with each step. It's a wonderful rocking motion that seems to go so well with the way the water thins out onto the sand, and then recedes, and then returns to wash your feet with its salty foam.

The ocean air feels so pleasant on your skin, and the smells of the ocean and scents of the blossoming trees nearby are softly intoxicating, beginning to make you a little drowsy. Soon you come to your cottage, open the screen door, and sit on the edge of the bed looking out at the sea and the sky.

A walk along the beach is used as a way of helping the listener wind down for the night. Lots of tactile cues are included: heels sinking into the sand, rocking motion, wet feet, the air on your skin. And then the sense of smell.

The first stars have begun to come out, and you take some time to just sit here, and watch them appear, one by one, as the last light of day fades, and the sky darkens to a deep velvet. Perhaps there's the sliver of the new moon, set just so, not far above the horizon.

You're in bed now, feeling your body relax from the day. Beginning with your feet, allow all the tension to go out of them now. They've worked hard for you all day, and deserve a rest. And so the relaxation in your feet begins to find its way into your ankles, your calves, and your knees. And now relax your upper legs, your hips, and your buttocks. And feel this relaxation flowing up into your abdomen and lower back, and your upper back and chest. And feel this peaceful, relaxing feeling flowing down your arms, into your hands, and out your fingertips. And then up into your neck, head and face.

Another full body relaxation. This time I've grouped body parts into threes, and changed the first part of each sentence slightly.

Now your whole body is perfectly calm, relaxed, and ready for sleep. And just to make sure there's nothing left between you and a gentle full night's rest, imagine that the very top of your head opens, and out float any thoughts that might still be trapped inside, to find their way into the beautiful, starry night sky, far above the sea, and drift out of sight. Now you're all clear. Don't forget to close the top of your head!

Why not have a little fun?

Soon you'll be sound asleep, off on a peaceful journey into dreamland that will carry you all the way through until morning. So as you continue to listen to the waves outside, begin to follow your breath, and inwardly say the words soft... sleep... deep... peace... soft... sleep... deep... peace... soft... sleep... deep... peace...

And finally the rhyming words, "soft, sleep, deep, peace" are repeated in a hypnotic way, and gradually fade into the background sound of ocean waves. The narrated portion of this program is less than 15 minutes, but the ocean wave sound continues for another half hour.

THE MIND-BODY CONNECTION FOR HEALING: IMMUNE SUPPORT

Here's a guided meditation that capitalizes on the mind-body connection to help boost a sense of wellness and well-being, and the immune system as a result.

Make yourself comfortable, and close your eyes. Take a slow deep breath, and let go of any tension, as you feel yourself sinking into the surface you're resting on, becoming still more comfortable and relaxed. Take another slow, deep breath, and release your thoughts, letting them drift far away. And take another slow, deep breath, and know that in this moment, all is well.

Imagine you're surrounded by a bubble of light, clear and perfect, and within this bubble you're becoming lighter, and lighter. Soon you're so light that you begin to float up, into the air, though the ceiling, and into a clear blue sky. Safe within your bubble you float and drift across lush forests, mountain meadows, and peaceful lakes and streams that mirror the sky above.

That is a classic "bubble of light" transition, used in some form in many, many guided meditations. Key words include "lighter, float, drift, clear, safe, peaceful."

> Nestled in the countryside below you can see a weathered old house with an expansive, rambling garden, and you find yourself drifting gently down toward it. Soon you softly come to rest in the middle of the garden, by a bubbling fountain. Have a seat at the edge of the fountain, and enjoy this lovely setting, landscaped with hedges, colorful flower beds, and leafy old shade trees here and there. The sound of the fountain's splashing water makes a soothing background to the day. Take a few moments to enjoy the feeling of peace and comfort here.

The setting for this meditation is a "weathered old house" and its garden. Every guided meditation doesn't have to be in a meadow, or on a beach. Keep your imagination open and consider new possibilities. For the recording I used a garden hose to capture a fountain sound.

> Although it seemed as if you were the only person here today, soon you begin to notice a few others walking along the paths, or seated on benches, quietly enjoying the garden.

> Someone comes and sits beside you, and their company feels most welcome. And as if it were the most natural thing in the world, they offer you their hand. And as soon as you take their hand in yours, you feel a flood of positive energy, as if you were receiving a transfusion of love, filling you from head to foot. Take time to receive this loving energy, as it continues to flow into you, clearing away any darkness, and leaving you fully alive.

Illness can bring a sense of isolation, and isolation can contribute to illness. So in this program about the immune system and wellbeing, I brought in the idea of a caring individual "lending a hand." Sometimes it's easier to imagine getting a boost from someone else, than receiving it out of thin air, although I've used that idea too.

> Now listen more closely to the fountain, and you'll notice its gentle splashing sound seems to resonate within your body. The sound is creating a healing resonance, clearing, brightening,

and strengthening your system. And as this occurs, it also clears your mind of any thoughts of weakness, hardship, or struggle concerning your health, giving you a clean mental slate. Take a few moments to experience this, and simply enjoy the feelings it brings.

The notion of clearing and healing coming to us from flowing water and/or light is one that is often used in guided imagery. I've used it in quite a few programs from my very earliest ones (The Healing Waterfall) to the most recent. There is something very relatable and accessible to this idea.

> The water itself has still more healing for you to experience. So if you wish, remove your shoes, turn around on the comfortable edge of the fountain and place your feet in the water, which you'll find is the perfect temperature, and very refreshing. Experience the healing energy as it flows into your feet and ankles, and gently flows up into your calves and knees.

> And now it flows into your upper legs, hips, and reproductive organs.

> This positive energy finds its way into your abdomen and lower back.

> And it flows into your upper back and chest.

> The healing energy of the fountain finds its way into all your internal organs, going where ever needed.

> Now feel it flowing into your shoulders and arms, into your hands and out your fingertips. And finally, it makes its way into your head and face, filling your eyes, ears, nose, mouth and brain.

> Now healing energy is circulating throughout your entire system, bringing strength and support where ever needed.

Here's another gradual full body progression. It's very similar to the one in Sleep Well Tonight (above), but this time with the notion of healing energy flowing through as opposed to simply relaxing.

> Your body, mind and emotions are adjusting to this higher vibration,

letting go of old patterns and programs, and stepping up to a new level of wellness.

As you continue to enjoy this positive transformation, listen to the following affirmations, and allow them find their way deep within you:

My mind is at peace, and my body is relaxed.

Light fills my body, mind and emotions, and I'm flooded with good health.

My body is a miraculous instrument, working in perfect harmony.

I am healthy and strong, and receive everything I need.

I enjoy a healthy mental diet of good, positive thoughts

I easily adjust to life's challenges with flexibility, and bounce back better than ever.

Life naturally flows throughout my system, feeding my body and mind with vibrant energy.

My body is naturally in tune with nature and the world around me, and operates in perfect harmony.

See the section on Affirmations, in Chapter 1, Writing Your Script.

It will soon be time to bring this journey to a close. But first, take a moment to thank yourself forgiving yourself this gift.

Bring your awareness gently back to your physical surroundings. Take your time, and when you're ready, open your eyes, and feel awake, alert, and refreshed.

GRIEF HEALING: SAYING GOODBYE

This is a guided meditation about connecting with a loved one who has passed over. The overall tone of this program is one of sensitivity and warmth, as it's really about helping the listener grieve and come to terms with their loss.

I'll use this program to illustrate examples of ways we can "hedge" our bets" with the listener, helping them avoid any sense of failure in using the meditation.

> Make yourself comfortable, and close your eyes. Take a slow deep breath, and let go of any tension, as you feel yourself sinking into the surface you're resting on, becoming still more comfortable and relaxed. Take another slow, deep breath, and release your thoughts, letting them drift far away. And take another slow, deep breath, and know that in this moment, all is well.
>
> Bring your awareness into your heart center, the energy center in the middle of your chest, and notice a softness there. Imagine all of the energy you've sent out into the world lately coming gently back home to your heart, helping you to feel more whole, and more complete. Quietly receive this energy, and know that for now, it's OK to simply be here, relax, and receive.
>
> Bring yourself more fully into your heart, as if you were standing there now, inside a cozy room. Soon, you'll notice a doorway, and as you walk through it, you'll find yourself in a setting that might be a very good place to visit with the one you've lost. This may be a place you both knew, or perhaps it's a beautiful place in nature you would both enjoy, like a quiet beach, or a mountain meadow. Take a moment to look around, and let your surroundings become more real to you, as you notice the colors, shapes, and sounds here.

As you can see, I've broken my own rule here about specifying and describing a specific scene for the listener. Instead I've asked them to pick a place they and their departed friend might enjoy together. Here I'm using this as a way of helping them to begin thinking more deeply about their friend. And, there's a good chance that choosing a special place they used to meet will enhance and enrich the "meeting" that's to come.

> Begin to call to mind things you and the one you've lost may have done together, or things you talked about, and before long, he or she will come more fully into your awareness, as you begin to see them, hear their voice, or simply feel their presence. Take a few moments to just be with them, together once again.

Any time we ask the listener to conjure up a specific image, hear a message, or imagine something unspecified, we're taking a risk—we risk the dreaded "I didn't get anything" response. Not everyone has an active or vivid imagination, and there's always the possibility that they may draw a blank. So in doing guided imagery we try to keep things open ended, and avoid triggering any sense of failure on the listener's part. In the paragraph above, we cover as many of the bases as possible. If the listener doesn't experience a full-on visit from their departed friend, chances are they will at least be able to conjure as sense of their "presence."

> As you continue to spend time here with the one you've lost, take this opportunity to say whatever you wish. This can be as simple as telling them what it's been like for you since they left; it might be things you've wanted to get off your chest for some time; or you may just want to express your love by telling them what they've meant to you. Take some time for this now.

> Now it's time to hear what they have to say to you. All you need do is quietly listen, feel, and receive. You may experience their words, thoughts, or felt communication, or there may simply be a quiet feeling of peace. Take some time for this now.

Here again we avoid the possibility of "failure," by making it OK to simply have a quiet feeling of peace.

> If there is anything you would like to know or hear from your loved one now, this would be a good time to ask. Take a few moments to ask, listen, and receive.

> Imagine that the two of you now stand facing one another, as you look into each other's eyes, and open your hearts. Take some time now, as best as you can, to be together, and give and receive love.

Another qualifier phrase: "as best as you can…"

> Although it's not easy to lose a loved one, you can and will go on with life. And although you will never see them again physically, your love for them will live on, and in your own perfect timing you'll adjust to life in a new way. Goodbye can mean different things at different times, so say the goodbye that's right for you, 45

just now. And if you can, let your loved one know that they are free to go on with their journey into love. Ask for a sphere of light to be placed around them, to help guide them on their way.

And another: "if you can…" By saying these kinds of qualifiers, we make it OK for the listener, no matter what their experience may be. There's no failure.

And, ask for a sphere of light to be placed all around you, and this experience, so that all the positive benefits will stay with you, and anything that you've released can be left behind. Take a moment to thank yourself forgiving yourself this gift.

It's time to bring your awareness gently back to your physical surroundings. Take your time, and when you're ready, open your eyes, and feel awake, alert, and refreshed.

CONNECTING WITH A SPIRITUAL FIGURE: VISITING SAINT FRANCIS

Here is a script written to help the listener have a vivid experience of an historical spiritual figure. Writing this script included a combination of research and inspiration.

Make yourself comfortable, and close your eyes. Take a slow deep breath, and let go of any tension in your body, as you settle into a more relaxed posture. Feel yourself dropping down from your mind into your body. Feel the weight of your body sinking into the surface you're resting on, as you become still more comfortable and relaxed.

Imagine you're walking in a beautiful mountain meadow, along a path by a quiet stream. It's a late summer morning, and the air is soft and warm. You can smell wildflowers blooming, and the plants along the water's edge, and as you walk along you can feel the soft ground beneath your footsteps.

Birds are singing to each other in the nearby trees, and you hear the sound of water running over the smooth, copper colored rocks on the streambed. A feeling of peace seems to encompass everything here, and you feel it begin to it settle over you as well.

Breath this peaceful feeling in, deeply and slowly now, and let it find its way everywhere within you.

It's always easiest to write from one's own experience. There is a monastery complex not far from my home, with a river bordering one side of the property. The two paragraphs above are actually my impression of a walk along that river. I jotted down my remembrances, including sight, sound, smell, and touch, and then fiddled with the words until something poetic emerged. As usual, I did some final run-throughs by reading out loud, to make sure the script would flow easily off the tongue.

As you continue to walk along this path, you sense the warm, familiar presence of an old friend, someone kind and gentle, and you have the unmistakable feeling he's come especially to see you. As he draws nearer, you feel your spirit lighten, and your heart open. And now, as if it were the most natural thing in the world, you feel Francis's hand resting gently on your shoulder, as you walk together along the path.

When we're introducing someone or something new in a guided meditation, it helps if we can find a way to bring them in gradually. In this case rather than simply saying something like "Francis is walking along side you now," I introduced him first by saying "you sense the warm, familiar presence…" Then "he draws nearer." Finally, "you feel Francis's hand resting gently on your shoulder." Although I gradually brought in Francis' presence with the sense of touch, one might do something similar with sound or sight. You could have the person first appear as a soft light form, and then come into focus. Or hear a sound like water flowing that gradually turns into their speaking voice, to offer two examples.

Francis has the touch of an older, wiser, and most compassionate brother. Of someone who's experienced tremendous joy, profound sadness, and most of all, a deep and constant bond of love with God the Creator. And by his hand upon your shoulder you know that he's here to share that bond of love with you.

One thing leads seamlessly into another: I used his touch as a way of developing the idea of his presence with you, into the reason for 47 his visit.

Turn and face Francis, and allow his presence to fill you. As more song birds come to visit, one by one, in the grass and trees nearby, you can feel Francis' love, and the grace surrounding him, growing stronger, expanding, and touching your heart.

Something within you stirs awake, and you know that this visit, this experience, is a doorway through which Francis' love, and God's grace, are coming into your life, to grow and blossom, like flowers in the meadow. Take some time to feel Francis' love for you now, and allow the grace that surrounds him to also surround and fill you.

Walking further along the path with Francis, you now begin to notice things differently. Everything in the meadow seems to have become enchanted with love and beauty. Colors have taken on a soft luster. The river seems to be alive and shining with light. The bird songs have grown sweeter and more innocent, and a light breeze has set the grasses and flowers swaying in unison, as if they were all listening to a song.

Francis guides you over to the stream, and the two of you sit side by side, your bare feet resting in the cool water. As you sit, look around and notice God's incredible handiwork. At your feet a few fish dart here and there in the gentle current. A butterfly visits a flower on the bank. A rabbit hops by on the opposite side of the stream, and takes a moment to sniff the air. Everywhere before you is the beauty of Creation, the world in which you are so intimately connected. This is God's world, and you are God's most precious creation. And in this moment, you know what Francis knows, that God's love lives within you always, now and forever.

The four paragraphs above were formed from a combination of what I researched about Francis, and my intuition about how his presence might influence us today.

The stream has become a luminous current of heavenly light, and it flows around your feet, lifting your spirit, clearing your mind, and healing your body. Ask now, in deepest prayer, that you be helped to release any anything that stands between you and your greater awakening, and open to the fullness of God's grace.

The idea of water turning into light is one that I've used more than once in spiritually oriented or healing oriented guided meditations. There's no reason you shouldn't use this idea in your writing too if you like, in your own words.

In answer to your prayer, waves of love flow from the Creator toward you and Francis, bringing blessings beyond measure. Take some time to breathe deeply, and receive.

As you continue to sit together, Saint Francis asks you to pray with him. Together, you say the following prayer, and you allow its meaning to go deep within you.

Lord, make me an instrument of your peace
Where there is hatred, let me sow love
Where there is injury, pardon
Where there is doubt, faith
Where there is despair, hope
Where there is darkness, light
And where there is sadness, joy.

Oh, Divine Master, grant that I may not so much seek to be consoled, as to console;
To be understood, as to understand
To be loved, as to love
For it is in giving that I receive
In pardoning that I am pardoned
And it is in dying that I am born to eternal life

If there is anything that has been troubling you, take a few moments to share it with Saint Francis now. With his kind, wise eyes full of compassion, he sees you, understands all you've gone through, and knows who you truly are, beyond all the trappings of your worldly existence. Allow him to comfort you in whatever way he feels is best, as you receive his blessing, through his words, his touch, or his gaze.

As usual, I tried to leave the door open for the listener's experience to be whatever it may be, by saying "through his words, his touch, or his gaze."

> It will soon be time to bring this journey to a close, so take a few moments to thank Francis for his love, and if you wish, ask him to remain with you in your heart over the coming days.

> Take your time, and when you're ready, bring your awareness gently back to your physical surroundings.

> Bring with you all you have learned, and when you're ready, open your eyes, and feel awake, alert, and refreshed.

DECISION MAKING: ROAD FORK PROCESS

This is a guided meditation from my online course, *Develop Your Psychic & Intuitive Ability*, also known as *Intuition Retreat*. It turns up late in the course, after a lot of ground work has already been laid.

> Make yourself comfortable, and close your eyes. Take a deep breath, and let go of any tension in your body, as you settle into a more relaxed posture. Feel yourself dropping down from your mind into your body. Feel the weight of your body sinking into the surface you're resting on, as you become still more comfortable and relaxed.

> Take a few moments to call upon your team, your guidance system, to assist you through this inner process, for your highest good.

"Your team, your guidance system" has previously been established in the course to include higher consciousness, spirit guides, angels, and so on. Prior to doing this exercise, the student was advised to consider a question about a decision they might need to make, to prepare for this meditation.

> Bring to mind a question involving two or more choices you'd like to consider, and pose the question to your guidance system. The information, energy and direction that comes to you through the rest of this process will address that question, or possibly cover a wider view than one your question represents. Set the question

aside now, relax your mind, and drop down once again into your body.

I've allowed the listener to engage the question with their intellect, essentially send it up to higher consciousness, and then set it aside to drop down deeper, getting the intellect once again out of the way.

> Imagine you're walking down a path, one that you may have been walking upon for some time. There's a familiar quality to the environment here, the air, the scenery, and even the rhythm of your footsteps are comfortable and natural for you, and you feel well within your element. And as you continue to walk, you realize that there's also a sense of protection surrounding you. Your team is with you as you go, and even though you're not always aware of their presence, they are always aware of you. They continually monitor your progress, and offer gentle support, guidance, and direction whenever necessary.

"Even though you're not always aware of their presence, they are always aware of you" is another way of failure-proofing the program, as discussed earlier.

> Glance behind you for a moment, and you'll see that your path extends far into the distant past, so far it disappears. And as you face forward again, you can see it also extends far into the future, surrounded ahead by a glow of golden light. Notice that as you continue to walk forward along this path there's no particular hurry or urgency. In fact, you can walk as slowly as you care to, taking in every bit of scenery along the way, or move more quickly if you wish, covering lots of ground in just an instant. Either way it's entirely up to you, and no matter where you are upon this path, there's always rich opportunity to enjoy yourself and explore the world around you. Every point along the way contains all the ingredients you need to guide you to your next step, and your next. And at each step you're more and more deeply supported in love.

The above paragraph includes suggestions that the listener can choose to adopt if appropriate. These suggestions are about setting aside worry, knowing that all is well, enjoying the journey rather than being preoccupied with the destination. However, those ideas are not spelled out specifically, because they might be too readily rejected should they bump up against certain beliefs. Instead they are alluded to in a more subtle way, and can be taken in as needed.

> As you continue walking, you begin to notice a fork in the path up ahead of you, like one of the many, many forks you've taken leading to where you're now, and like those you'll continue to take as you move forward. Some forks allow you to take more scenic routes, offer a different view, or lead you to join with others along your path. And all forks eventually lead to your greater growth and bring you closer to your source, the source of all that is.

In the last sentence I've made a conscious choice to insert my own philosophical belief here, that life is for growth and learning. You may or may not wish to do that, depending upon your audience.

> Imagine that the fork ahead of you represents two or more choices you might be faced with currently in your life. You'll have the opportunity now to experiment with these choices by traveling a ways down each direction, and experiencing what it might be like. And so, with the presence of your team with you as they always are, begin to face one direction of this fork and walk toward it.

> Notice the feeling within you as you approach this fork. Does the energy of this direction seem to support you? As you continue to move forward and step upon this section of the path, become aware of any changes you feel within you, and whether they feel positive and uplifting. If it feels as if there's a sense of struggle here, notice whether there's also a quality of potential within it, or if it seems as if any reward would be scant. Do you feel comfortable here, or challenged in a positive way? What do you notice about the scenery here? Do you find it interesting and engaging, or does it all seem a bit too familiar? As you explore further, what sounds or words seem to come to mind about this path? Is there something about this path that makes you want to go further and further, or would you rather be where you were before you set off on this direction. Take a few moments to

explore here.

Here we come to the core of this process, in which the listener gets to try out or rehearse different possible choices ahead. By asking so many questions, there's a risk of bringing the listener too far back up into their intellect. To help avoid that, and because relying on feelings is a big part of the overall course the program comes from, I've emphasized noticing how things feel.

You've gotten plenty of information for now about that direction, so go back to the point at which you began to turn off, and face another direction instead, walking toward it.

Notice the feeling within you as you approach this fork. Does the energy of this direction seem to support you? As you continue to move forward and step upon this section of the path, become aware of any changes you feel within you, and whether they feel positive and uplifting. If it feels as if there's a sense of struggle here, notice whether there's also a quality of potential within it, or if it seems as if any reward would be scant. Do you feel comfortable here, or challenged in a positive way? What do you notice about the scenery here? Do you find it interesting and engaging, or does it all seem a bit too familiar? As you explore further, what sounds or words seem to come to mind about this path? Is there something about this path that makes you want to go further and further, or would you rather be where you were before you set off on this direction. Take a few moments to explore here.

All exactly the same content, looking at a different choice.

Now go back to the point at which you began to turn toward this direction. If you have still more paths you'd like to explore, you may do that, by stopping the recording and coming back to this point when you've tried out each direction. If not let's go on.

Suggesting stopping the recording to do more is not an ideal solution. But there's no way of knowing in a recording how much the listener needs to explore. So, there it is.

As you stand upon your path now, imagine you're surrounded   53 by a clear bubble of light, and allow your team to lift you gently into the air, so you're able to get a bird's eye view of your path, including the fork before you. As you lift higher, you may notice that there are in fact lots and lots of forks in your path, many that you've taken, and many still to come, and almost all of them seem to be glowing with promise. Allow your team to lift you still higher, until the landscape below fades far into the distance, and you settle into a beautiful landing area, radiant with light, high above.

This is a place where your soul is quite comfortable, your entire being is open and expansive, and you're able to easily communicate with your team, who are gracefully surrounding you now. Take some time here, as they transmit to you any new information or energetic adjustment you may need, to better prepare you for the road ahead. Set aside any thoughts or concerns about your future, and simply receive their blessing, knowing that the way is paved before you.

The process of looking at choices set forth above may have been stressful. So I've given the listener the opportunity to "rise above." There the idea is seeded once again that it's all part of the walk of life, and all is well. Finally, an opening for receiving a "blessing" from higher support.

Remain here as long as you wish, and when you're ready, bring with you all that you've learned, and gently and gradually bring your awareness back to your physical surroundings. Take your time, and when you're ready, open your eyes and feel awake, alert and refreshed.

I often included an ending note such as "bring with you all you've learned," or "let all the benefits of this experience stay with you," as I have done here. This helps to bridge the insights and good feelings gained within the meditation into the listener's daily life.

PERSONAL GROWTH: GOOD BOUNDARIES

This guided imagery program was written to help change a deep psychological pattern: personal boundary issues. In this meditation, the listener finds herself in a primordial forest, and makes her way to an underground movie theater, a "theater of the mind." Once there she uses the screen to review and then rewrite incidents from her life where personal boundary issues came into play.

This meditation is a way of stepping back from everyday life, taking a good hard look at how a pattern plays out, and setting a clear intention to change the pattern. It's a model or template that could be applied to many other behavior patterns. There is also a good bit of informational content for the listener, mixed in.

Make yourself comfortable, and close your eyes. Take a slow deep breath, and let go of any tension in your body, as you feel yourself sinking into the surface you're resting on, becoming still more comfortable and relaxed. Take another slow, deep breath, and feel a sense of calm and peace begin to fill you, as you relax further. And take another slow, deep breath, and let your thinking begin wind down and smooth out.

Imagine you've been sleeping a deep, sound sleep for many hours, and you're just beginning to stir awake. And the first thing you notice, is that you're waking up on a soft bed of pine needles, on the ground, surrounded by ancient fir trees. It's just before dawn, and the air is quite cool, the light is dim, and there's a foggy mist in the air. You can smell the scent of pine, and the damp coolness of the earth. It's quiet, and any sound is blanketed by the mist. Everything is a palette of soft greens, browns, and grays.

Standing up, you begin to walk along a path through the trees, and you can feel the spongy ground beneath your feet. Perhaps you still feel a bit foggy from your sleep, but soon you come to a little spring, cup your hands to get a drink, and splash some of the cool, clear water on your face. Now you're beginning see the trees and plants that surround you more clearly.

Walking further along, you come to a small bunker with what appears to be a cellar door folded down into it. There's a little sign on the door, and looking more closely, you see that the sign has your name written upon it, followed by the words, *Enter To Wise Up*. Before you do enter, consider that you're about to gain 55 clarity on a pattern that has controlled and limited you, probably for many years. With this new clarity, you'll have the opportunity to make a change. But the choice to change your behavior will remain in your hands. Are you ready? It's time to find out.

Changing behavior patterns is not an easy or trivial pursuit. Dramatically setting up the listener, as in the paragraph above, is a simple but powerful technique to emphasize the importance of what's to come. It helps bring added focus to their experience.

Open the door. Before you are five stairs down to a landing, and you can see a soft light coming from the other side of the landing, at the bottom of the stairs.

As you step down onto the first step, take a moment to consider the following question: *What do I do for others that should be their responsibility to do themselves?*

As you step down to the second step, take a moment to consider this question: *In what situations do I give away my time, energy, money, to gain acceptance, love or appreciation?*

As you step down to the third step, consider this question: *In what ways do I leave my own center and ignore my own truth to try and get my physical or emotional needs met?*

As you step down to the fourth step, take a moment to consider this question: *What do I feel or believe about myself, that makes me willing to leave my center and ignore my own truth?*

And as you step down to the fifth step, take a moment to consider this question: *What situations do I allow to occur, or not take precautions to prevent, that result in my being abused, hurt or taken unfair advantage of?*

Here I've used the descending staircase as a metaphor for going deep into the subconscious mind, where behavior patterns live. I've used the steps as part of the setup to bring up details about the ways boundary issues effect the listener's life. We're digging in and bringing to the surface what needs to be looked at and released.

Step down to the landing, look through the doorway, and you'll see you've come to a small movie theater for an audience of one, with a comfortable chair, thick carpet, sloping walls with speakers set into them and a sleek movie screen at the front. Have a seat in the chair and make yourself at home, as the house lights dim, and the screen fills with the same words that appeared on the bunker door: your name, and just below it, the words, *Time To Wise Up*.

I like the idea of bringing informal, humorous, or colloquial language into an otherwise rather heavy program. Inserting a rueful catch-phrase like "Time To Wise Up" helps make the listener's experience more palatable, enjoyable, and memorable, and as a result, more effective.

The movie begins with a recent scene from your life, in which you were either taken advantage of or abused, or in which you took it upon yourself to do something for someone else that was not appropriate or healthy for you to be doing for them. Watch that scene unfold, and notice how your energy is effected in the movie, and how you feel.

Watch that scene again, and see, hear, and feel it with as much clarity as possible, as everything comes into sharper focus.

Watch that scene one more time, and this time notice the point at which you either made the decision to do what you did, or chose not to take action to stop it from happening. Notice whether you were conscious of the decision or choice, or if it seemed to happen without you even being aware of it.

Adult behavior patterns like allowing or inviting others to take unfair advantage are typically established in childhood. Once we're grown up they become second nature. Correcting habitual behavior requires first becoming aware of it. This guided meditation is all about bringing unconscious habitual patterns into awareness.

The next scene is one that's not quite so recent, and again it's one in which you were either taken advantage of or abused, or in which you took it upon yourself to do something for someone else that was not appropriate or healthy for you to be doing for them. Watch that scene unfold, and notice how your energy is effected in the movie, and how you feel.

Watch that scene again, and see, hear, and feel it with as much clarity as possible, as everything comes into sharper focus.

Watch that scene one more time, and this time notice the point at which you either made the decision to do what you did, or chose not to take action to stop it from happening. Notice whether you were conscious of the decision or choice, or if it seemed to happen without you even being aware of it.

We began with a present day example that might be easy to bring to mind, then went back in time to an earlier one that requires a little more digging to bring up.

The movie changes now, and goes back to a point in time to where the theme of your story seems to have its beginnings, probably in childhood. As you watch this part of the movie, remember that you are now all grown up, are safe and protected in this moment, and have all the resources of a fully grown adult to take good care of yourself. You're only watching this movie to gather information, and there's no need to re-experience your emotions from the past.

It should be obvious that we want to avoid re-triggering any past trauma. So the above paragraph has several cues to help the listener avoid that.

What were the circumstances that made you leave your center, take on responsibilities that shouldn't have been yours, do something for someone else that wasn't good for you to do, become the object of abuse, or to be taken advantage of?

Watch this scene just one more time, but this time, see your adult-self come into the scene to guide and protect your childhood self, either by helping you make a better decision, by physically protecting you, or by completely removing yourself from that situation, taking your childhood self to a safe place.

See yourself safe and protected, and take a deep breath. See and feel that situation completely surrounded and filled with healing light, of whatever color you and your childhood self would like. Take another deep breath, and allow all feelings of fear, anger, or sadness to be released into the healing light, as you recognize that this happened long ago, and it's past and finished. Today you're all grown up, and can take good care of yourself, just as you've just taken care of your childhood self, and today you have many more choices and opportunities to shape your life.

The next part of the movie will show you how to let go of old patterns from the past, and establish a more positive, healthier way of being.

See yourself standing alone in a favorite setting, a place of your choice that feels safe and comfortable, and you feel relaxed and free to be yourself. Imagine you're moving directly into that scene now, and as you stand, become aware of a column of light extending from the highest heavens, straight through you and deep into the earth, all the way to earth's core. As the light passes through you, it resonates especially in your heart center, merging with your own energy, and expanding outward. Focus in your heart, and you can feel a deep sense of connection and strength.

The "column of light" motif is one that I adapted from spirituality practices, and I use it in guided imagery for various kinds of healing and personal growth. The listener doesn't have to buy into the notion of spiritual light to gain support. They can benefit by simply playing along with the idea, allowing the imagery to help instill new feelings of confidence, comfort, wellness, and release of fear and sadness.

As the light continues to pass through you, you feel more and more centered, grounded, and whole. You are fully self-contained and content, complete unto yourself. A circular zone of protection seems to project out all around you, and you can see it expanding out from your feet, your heart and your head. This zone, and the column of light passing through you, represent your healthy boundary. It's both an energetic boundary and a physical one, and it comes from the center of your own being.

As you continue to stay centered, heart focused, and grounded, your energy becomes stronger, healthier, and more self-contained than ever.

Take some time to experience this inner connection, as you listen to the following affirmations, and allow them to resonate deep within.

I am centered, grounded, and connected inside, and know who I am.

I allow into my circle only those who are supportive of me and my life.

I take care of myself first, not selfishly but as my healthy personal responsibility.

I do things for others only when appropriate and supportive for everyone involved, including myself.

When I find myself faced with any person or situation that would threaten my safety, dignity, or wellbeing, I physically remove myself from that person or situation without delay, and go somewhere safe.

I look out for myself, and plan so my needs are covered, and I always have somewhere safe to be.

I choose to be only with those who respect my healthy boundaries, and insist that all others go their own way.

I am worthy of love, respect, and appreciation, and find that within myself.

Watch yourself on the screen, centered within your zone of protection, and notice how vital and strong your own energy is. Notice that when you reach out to someone else while centered, your energy stays strong, and your light stays bright. But when you reach to someone from sadness or a sense of lack, you move out of your circle, and your energy drops, and darkens. As soon as you leave your center to try to gain satisfaction, you cannot be truly satisfied. But when you remain centered, you have the opportunity to find the love, acceptance, and support you're looking for within yourself. At that point you can begin to attract people to you who will honor, appreciate, and respect who you are.

As you can see, there is quite a bit of informational content mixed in with the guided imagery in this program. Even the affirmations are intended to be instructive as well as motivational. When the content leans toward information, it will tend to pull the listener into the intellect, away from the deeper relaxation zone we typically target in guided meditation. That can be OK, depending upon the purpose of the program. And while this one is largely instructional, the guided meditation format helps the listener take in the content in a deeper way than they might if they were just listening to an self-help audiobook.

Take some time to watch yourself on screen, as you experiment staying in your center and connecting with yourself and others in a healthy way; as well as seeing what happens when you do the opposite, and leave your center to try to gain someone else's approval or sympathy. Notice how your energy changes, what leaves you feeling drained, and what supports you.

Now take a few moments to consider what changes you might need to make in your life, to create the opportunity to develop good healthy boundaries. What situations would you need to avoid, and what would you need to cultivate? What relation- ships would you need to change or diminish, and how would you change them?

Projecting into the future is a technique I often use as part of guided meditations designed to help change patterns. It takes the listener from a place of looking at what doesn't work to a place of what steps they can take to make the change. In some cases I'll suggest looking ahead at specific intervals; next day, next week, next month, and so on.

It's almost time to bring this inner journey to a close. So gather together anything you have learned, that you'd like to bring with you, and plan to write about your experience and any changes you'll need to make, after the meditation. Gradually bring your awareness back into your body, and your physical surroundings. Take your time, and when you're ready, open your eyes, and feel awake, alert, and refreshed. Pick up your pen and paper, and write about your experience now, while it's still fresh in your mind.

I'm a big proponent of journaling, especially immediately after meditation. I often include the suggestion for journaling at the end of a program, particularly when a lot of information has been conveyed.

METAPHOR & WORDPLAY: FINDING HOPE

This program was part of a series of guided meditations I wrote to correspond to the 38 Bach Flower Essences, and the mental and emotional conditions they address. One of those conditions is hopelessness. The Bach Flowers work quite well on their own, but I wanted to create some supplemental programs to help people process things in a more conscious way.

To be honest, when I began writing this script I thought it was a reach to expect a guided meditation to help with hopelessness, and frankly I still do. There are so many potential external, situational factors that can contribute to hopelessness, way beyond what a narrated program could address.

Yet the outlook of hope is itself an internal condition, so I decided to rise to the challenge, and take a crack at making something helpful. In writing this program I turned to metaphor and wordplay, hoping to tickle the listener's unconscious mind into playing along. The program concludes with a series of pertinent affirmations, and directions to the listener for taking steps to change their outward situation as needed.

> Make yourself comfortable, and close your eyes. Take a slow deep breath, and let go of any tension, as you feel yourself sinking into the surface you're resting on, becoming still more comfortable and relaxed. Take another slow, deep breath, and release your thoughts, letting them drift far away. And take another slow, deep breath, and know that in this moment, all is well.
>
> Imagine you've been searching for a dear friend of yours, someone you've known and loved for many years, named Hope. You and Hope had some wonderful times together, and when you're with her, you always feel uplifted, and willing to try new things. But lately you've been separated, and you've had trouble finding your friend Hope, and you've become quite sad.

I personalized hope into an old friend the listener is searching for.

> You thought you might find Hope in the north central US, in Minnesota, because there's a city there called New Hope. And so you travel by airplane, and train, and then bus, and finally arrive in New Hope.
>
> You have no idea where to begin, so you simply start going door to door, asking for your friend, Hope. And at each house you're told "No, there's no Hope here, no Hope at all", and "No, they don't know where to find your friend Hope."

The script actually pushes further into the feeling of hopelessness here, to bring it into high relief. The idea is to make the listener more acutely aware of the condition, in order to then make a shift.

> And so you decide to rest. You find a park, with a grassy lawn, and some comfy old benches, and you settle down, close your eyes and take a snooze for a while. Soon you're dreaming about going door to door, finding no Hope. And in the dream you're sitting on the curb, and see a car go by. And for just a moment, just before the car passes out of sight you think you see Hope riding along in the front seat.
>
> That's when you wake up. And who do you suppose is sitting right next to you, on that park bench, in New Hope Minnesota? It's Hope of course, just like you remember her.
>
> She's looking at you, and smiling, just as lovely and friendly as ever. Take a moment to catch up with her, find out where she's been, and get reacquainted. You might want to tell her how you've been looking for her, all the things you've tried, and how hard it's been. She'll listen, understand, and help you to lighten up. Do this for a moment now.

Now we shift gears:

> Now that you've found hope, consider one thing you can do, perhaps something you can look into, someone you can talk to, or something you can try, to help your current situation. Take a moment now to imagine that this meditation is over, and you are

taking those steps.

Listen to the following affirmations, and allow them to resonate, deep within.

I am opening to new possibilities, and allowing life to fill me with enthusiasm.

I am allowing life to breathe new energy into me, and am being lifted.

I am hoping for the best possible outcome, and am embracing all that is good.

I am taking charge of my attitude, looking forward, and turning toward the light.

I am finding hope and encouragement at the core of my being, and making a choice to feel optimistic.

It will soon be time to bring this inner journey to a close. But first, take a moment to thank yourself, forgiving yourself this gift.

Let all the benefits of this experience stay with you, and you gently bring your awareness gently back to your physical surroundings. Take your time, and when you're ready, open your eyes, and feel awake, alert, and refreshed.

So can a program like this actually help with hopelessness?

Often it takes a combination of things to address emotional issues and produce a shift. In the course of trying to heal, a patient or client might see one or more counselors over a period of time, and make changes to their diet, exercise, occupation, and social situation. It can sometimes be hard to pinpoint one thing that made the difference, and it's more likely that a combination of many things will ultimately work.

I have not received enough feedback about this program to know how helpful it might be for its intended purpose. But my sense is that a program like this one could at least be one part of the overall picture. Perhaps just hearing one of the affirmations in a program like this one might help push the listener to the top of their mountain.

All we can do is try!

TRANSFORMING THE HEART: RELEASING BITTERNESS, OPENING TO LOVE

This is quite a long guided meditation, filled with enough concepts and content for two or three programs.

> Make yourself comfortable, and close your eyes. Take a slow deep breath, and let go of any tension, as you feel yourself sinking into the surface you're resting on, becoming still more comfortable and relaxed. Take another slow, deep breath, and release your thoughts, letting them drift far away. And take another slow, deep breath, and know that in this moment, all is well.
>
> Imagine you've been sound asleep and dreaming, and in your dream you're standing on the edge of a vast desert. All you can see before you are scrub brush, rocks and sand. A hot, dry wind blows across the arid landscape, and the sky holds only a single, small white cloud drifting overhead.

Not all guided imagery has to be sweet and happy. The paragraph above is intentionally bleak, to help set a specific tone for what's to come. The above paragraph and the next several encapsulate the listener's situation, the reason they have come to this guided meditation for help. Rather than beginning with happy content to try to mollify the listener, my aim was to bring their problem fully into their awareness. Dramatizing this sets the listener up for a more impactful resolution.

> As you stand here, you're aware of a need for change within you; a need to release old wounds, let go of negative patterns of thinking and behavior, and embrace a more fertile and life-affirming way. The desert before you represents the past, and the future is quite unknown. In order to release the past you'll need to be open to new possibilities, and most of all, allow your attitude to change toward whatever may come your way. This may not be easily done, but the time has come to step forward on a new path.

Changing one's attitude is in fact not always an easy task. Sometimes it's good to say that, rather than set the listener up for failure by 65 implying it's going to be a breeze. In this case it's helpful to let them know that while this can be a new beginning, change may take time.

Look down to your left, and you'll find a weathered old book. Pick it up, and you'll see it has your name on the cover, following by the subtitle, "Chronicle of Disappointments." As you open the book, you'll see that its pages all appear to be blank, but you soon find them filling with words describing every hurt feeling, disappointment, betrayal, and injury you've ever received. The wind comes up and blows the pages from the front to the back of the book. All your bitterness is here in this one volume.

Look down to your left, and you'll find a shovel. Pick it up, and without hesitation, dig a deep hole in the soft desert ground, and bury the book. Your time of bitterness is over, and this marks the end. Take a moment to let go, and say goodbye to this part of your life.

Having summarized and put a fine point on the current situation and the past, next comes a metaphor for a new beginning.

Reach into your pocket, and you'll find a small envelope, containing just one seed. Place the seed in the soil, over where you just buried the book, and cover it with earth. Knowing this fragile seed represents your future, take a moment to reach into the deepest recesses of your heart, connect with divinity in the best way you're able, and say a prayer for the growth and survival of this seed.

How far should we to lean toward spiritual references with guided meditation? If we know that our listener has a spiritual or religious orientation, it can be especially helpful to bring that in as a resource. If they don't have such beliefs, it can be a distraction. So it's a judgement call based on what we know about our audience. More on this a bit further ahead.

Now the sky clouds over, thunder rolls in, and rain begins pouring down, drenching you, and covering the ground as far as you can see. The rain continues on, until it begins pooling up all around you, turning the desert landscape into a shallow lake. There's nothing more for you to do here now, and as you turn to leave, your dream changes.

The next several paragraphs extend far into new age spirituality territory. This works well within the context of this particular program, assuming the listener is willing to entertain the ideas. One potentially helpful thing about spirituality is that it suggests the concept that there is a greater power at work than ourselves, loosely similar to invoking one's Higher Power in 12-Step programs. Not only can there be comfort in such a belief, but it can help introduce optimism and set up an openness for change.

As an alternative to spiritual references you might reference the word "life" instead of "God," and call upon metaphors from nature. Talk about the way life evolves, renews, and reinvents itself, the persistence and resourcefulness of animals, or the way some trees can take root and thrive in even the poorest soil.

> The rain stops, clouds part, the sky turns blue, and you're lifted into the air. Higher and higher you go, until you find yourself far above the land, then traveling farther still into a heavenly realm, full of stars, clouds, and crystalline shapes. Soon you find yourself on a treatment table in a sacred chamber of healing. You're being attended by a small, elite group of healers; the most caring, nurturing, and expert beings you've ever experienced. The feeling of safety, comfort, and support for you here is beyond anything you could imagine. You feel so completely open to receive what's being offered, that it almost seems as if all the molecules that make up your body are opening and expanding, allowing in the healing energies, releasing anything within you that no longer supports your growth.

> One of the healers places hands on your head, and you feel your mind open, expand, and let go. The healer begins speaking to you telepathically, and says:

> "Dear one, like so many on Earth, your path has led through painful experiences that have caused you to close down and become bitter. But please understand that this is only temporary. We are here to help set your course back toward wholeness and

peace. Our job is not to erase your dark memories, but to bring light into those places within you, loosen blocks, and soften you so you can begin moving forward again. You need do nothing now but receive."

The idea of receiving love, energy, or healing without giving something in return is a challenging concept for some people. Many of us have been programmed to believe that we're not worthy, or that we need to participate somehow, or think about or control what we might receive. But being able to simply open to receive without doing anything else can pave the way toward emotional healing. It's an important step.

The healers come close and send rays of healing light streaming from their hands into your body. Light energies of all colors reach deep within, going wherever needed, touching stored grief, pain, and sadness. You spontaneously begin to shed tears that seem to come from a deep, ancient source within. Memories quickly surface and release, as all is in motion within you. Allow this process to unfold for some time, as you receive, let go, and receive more. [pause]

The healer's voice again resonates within your mind, saying "Your healing process has been set in motion, but you'll need to follow through in the physical world to complete the work. Go toward those who can help you move forward, and find the friends and experts who can best support you. Follow your heart, and let it lead to the ones you feel drawn to. You will be supported both in your world and from above as your path unfolds."

Perhaps you already have some idea about those who can help your healing process, whether they be counselors, teachers, healers or friends. Take a moment to consider who you would most like to connect with, and imagine yourself being with them now, receiving their support and guidance.

Here's another example of taking what is brought up in a meditation, and connecting that to the steps needed out in the world. Very often the work begun in a program like this needs follow-through to bring results. I like to seed the idea of taking such action in the program itself.

Your dream changes once again, and you return to the place where you planted the seed. But now the landscape bears no resemblance to the desert you saw earlier, having transformed into a rich, dense forest. You're standing at the edge of this forest, looking down a long, winding trail. It's late afternoon, and the light is soft. The air is warm, and as a breeze finds you, you can smell pine, the sweet scent of the forest floor, and the yellow buttercups and bluebonnets along the trail before you. The path beckons, and it feels like the perfect time for a walk, so you set off on your way.

The forest is quiet, and your steps are soft on the spongy ground. And as you walk along you're soon enveloped by a peaceful feeling of enchantment, slowing everything down, taking you deeper and deeper within.

Soon it feels as if you've entered another world, like a dream where the shapes and colors of the forest glow from within, coming gently alive.

Your path leads to a little stream, one you can easily step across, and you stop to look in at the clear water, the bright copper colored stones, and a little fish darting here and there in the current. So much has already happened today, yet you feel open to whatever this new leg of your journey holds for you, and welcome the discovery.

There's lots of rich imagery in the paragraphs above to set up for the next part of the meditation. But it's getting to be a long program! In fact, I could have broken this program up into more than one part. But I wanted to extend this one, so I put in the last sentence above. To help the listener continue on and receive more, I acknowledged that it's a lot, and included some encouragement for going on.

Your path winds its way through ancient firs and oaks tangled with vines, until you come upon a huge boulder in the shape of a human heart. Standing before this boulder, you take it in for a moment, and feel your own heart begin to open and expand in response, preparing for what's to come.

Imagery drawn from my own experience. In the paragraph above, I recalled a huge heart shaped boulder I've seen in the New Mexico landscape not far from my home. I recommend keeping a journal of anything you see or hear that might eventually find its way into your writing.

> Stepping quietly around the boulder, you discover a small clearing, a meadow filled with wild flowers and waving grass.

> Entering the clearing, you come upon a solitary deer, who immediately senses your presence, and looks up to face you. As your eyes meet, you're flooded with a sense of awe and wonder at the beauty of this creature. The deer is totally at home in this setting, as if he were an extension of the plants, trees, and even the air you're sharing. And in the deer's eyes, you don't see fear, but recognition, as if he were expecting you. You're here to learn something about yourself, and the deer is here to help you.

> Standing very still, you feel the unspoken connection between the two of you, and soon the deer begins speaking to you telepathically, as you hear his words resonate within your mind.

> "Reality is upside down. Although this may seem like a dream, I am very real. But in your life, what you think of as your problems are imaginary. Look: All around me are gifts: the trees, the moss on the rocks, the air, the water. You have gifts all around you also. Do you see them?"

The idea of encountering a talking/telepathic deer, and the sentence, "Reality is upside down," are designed to catch the listener's attention in a slightly disruptive way. When done gracefully, this can create an opening to allow in a positive suggestion, as follows.

> Take a moment to consider one situation in your life, and let the gifts surrounding it come into focus.

> The deer continues, "In winter, snow covers most of the ground, but I find a few leaves to eat, or I become very quiet and rest to conserve energy. I am humble and cooperative, and therefore can

live and appreciate this world; a world that offers me everything."

Take a moment to consider another situation in your life, and open to the awareness of how you might shift your attitude and come into greater cooperation, to better support yourself, appreciate your life, and enjoy what you've been given.

When you look again, you see that the deer has been joined by more deer, male and female, young and old.

Again you hear the deer speak, saying "Life is in motion behind every leaf and blade of grass, and others join you in perfect timing. Openness toward others brings happiness and peace."

Consider the people in your life, and your potential to open to receive love. What attitudes of bitterness, judgment, or separation might you now turn into acceptance, appreciation, and compassion? Take some time to imagine yourself letting go, opening, and making a deeper connection with the most important people in your life, perhaps even with some who are challenging.

It will soon be time to bring this journey to a close. But first, ask for a sphere of light to be placed all around you, and this experience, so that all the positive benefits will stay with you, and anything that you've released can be left behind.

Take a moment to thank yourself forgiving yourself this gift.

Bring your awareness gently back to your physical surroundings. Take your time, and when you're ready, open your eyes, and feel awake, alert, and refreshed.

REHEARSAL FOR SUCCESS: WINNING YOUR IDEAL JOB

A "rehearsal" meditation can be effective for any forthcoming event or encounter a listener feels apprehension about; or when successful performance is a concern. This program is a kind of rehearsal meditation written to prepare the listener for an interview for a coveted job.

Make yourself comfortable, and close your eyes. Take a slow deep breath, and let go of any tension, as you feel yourself sinking into the surface you're resting on, becoming still more comfortable and relaxed. Take another slow, deep breath, and release your thoughts, letting them drift far away. And take another slow, deep breath, and know that in this moment, all is well.

Consider your job skills, those you currently possess, as well as any you might be learning on your new job. Take a moment to envision yourself at your new job, applying those skills, and producing a positive outcome. Use your imagination to put yourself there and make it as real as you can.

The above paragraph and the next two are designed to help put the listener in touch with their sense of value and purpose, and pump them up in preparation for her meeting. As they imagine themself in the job they are applying for, the listener begins to take ownership of their skills and abilities, developing confidence.

Now bring to mind some of the key personal qualities you possess, things about you that will make a positive contribution to the business and people you'll be working with. For example, honesty, reliability, and consideration for others are things that create a positive atmosphere, and help get work done easily. Envision yourself at your new job, bringing out your personal qualities with positive results. Take a moment to use your imagination and make it as real as you can.

In an exercise like the one described in the paragraph above, it helps to be specific: "These are my talents, abilities, and ways I make a difference. This is what I bring to the table." Imagining a general sense of value would not be effective for providing the meaning and memory hooks needed to build self-esteem. We tend to take in and remember specifics.

Take a little longer to imagine yourself at your new job, as if you're already working there. Envision yourself coming to work, doing your job, interacting with others. Experience yourself fitting right in, feeling connected with that workplace and the people there. Make it as real in your imagination as you can, and get a good strong feeling of being a part of that work environment, bringing all your skills and personal qualities with you.

It's a popular notion that a good way to bring about a desired outcome is to imagine it is already happening. "I'm already in my new job, and it's real." The above paragraph and the one below put that concept to use.

> Now use your imagination to carry forward that feeling of connection with your new job directly into your job interview, so that while you're speaking with your interviewer, it feels as if you are already hired and working there. Imagine yourself in the interview session, being yourself, relaxed and comfortable, with all your skills and personal qualities present.

First we helped the listener feel a sense of ownership of the new job, and put her in touch with her skills and values. Now, armed with that positive sense of self, we bring her to the more challenging part of the meditation—the job interview.

> Take a series of slow, deep breaths now, breathing way down into your abdomen. And as you do, imagine you're also breathing deeply and slowly in your interview. Feel your feet on the floor. You're grounded and connected, relaxed and comfortable. Take some time to hold this focus now, simply focusing on being in your interview, comfortable and relaxed, grounded and connected.

The most important part of being interviewed, or being in any situation in which we need to be at our best, is being relaxed. When we're relaxed and comfortable, our interviewer is more likely to feel the same way.

> Imagine your conversation with your interviewer. You're being yourself, open and honest, not saying too little or too much. Take a moment to project into your interview, speaking about yourself clearly and openly, putting your best foot forward.

> Listen to the following affirmations, and allow them to resonate, deep within.

> *I take all the time necessary to prepare for my interview, so I'm confident and comfortable going in.*

> *I'm likable and easy to relate to.*

I connect easily with others.

When people meet me, they like me, and tend to quickly focus on my good qualities.

I have a natural ability to please people, and enjoy helping them get what they want.

I am confident in my abilities, and radiate ease and comfort.

I am honest and open about myself, my skills, and my qualities, saying what's important to put me in the best light possible.

I represent myself well, speak positively about myself, and saying just enough.

I already feel I'm a part of my new workplace, and have the job I've been looking for.

I like my interviewer, and he or she likes me.

It will soon be time to bring this journey to a close. But first, take a moment to thank yourself forgiving yourself this time and space to prepare for your next step.

Bring your awareness gently back to your physical surroundings. Take your time, and when you're ready, open your eyes, and feel awake, alert, and refreshed.

LEADING A SIMPLE MEDITATION PROCESS: SANCTUARY OF PEACE

Here is a guided meditation that simply helps listeners "meditate." There are lots of different kinds of meditation, some of which lend themselves to being "guided," and some not so much. Sanctuary of Peace offers the listener a "heart focus" meditation. This kind of meditation is a very simple process that could be summed up by the words, "focus in your heart and follow your breath." The challenge is that when we try to do that, we invariably end up back in our head, where we are more used to being. It takes a great deal of practice, repetition, and *encouragement* (from the word "cor," "coeur," or "heart") to gradually learn to stay focused in the heart.

So this guided meditation offers a series of prompts, with subsequent time to focus and refocus in the heart. Each period of focus time lasts a little longer. Interspersed are some encouraging statements, just enough to quiet the intellect, and redirect the listener toward the heart.

For some listeners, those who are able to go into the heart and stay there more easily, the encouraging statements in this program might actually be a distraction. For others they will be a helpful reminder. All of which is to say that it helps to know your audience, and adjust your narration accordingly.

But do keep in mind that when you publish any kind of guided meditation, or perform one live for a group, there will always be those who appreciate it because it suits them well, and others for whom it falls short, and experiences everywhere in between. And, what works for a listener at one point in time won't necessarily always fit them later. It's all down to the individual and where they happen to be in the moment. In guided meditation as in life, no one bats 1000!

And so with that, here is the script for Sanctuary Of Peace.

> Sit comfortably upright, so you can relax and go within, without falling asleep. Close your eyes, and take a slow, deep breath. Adjusting your breathing will allow you to more easily spend time within your sanctuary of peace, so continue to breathe deeply, and slowly, taking comfortably full breaths. Some of us tend to breathe using our chest, and others with our abdomen, but if you can, use your belly, allowing it to expand as you breathe in, and relax as you breathe out.

"Belly breathing" or "yoga breathing" as it is also called, helps us fill the lungs more fully, and relax more deeply, than using only the chest and upper part of the lungs.

> Bring your focus into your heart center, in the center of your chest. This will help you relax your mind, wind down, un-busy yourself, and begin to enter your sanctuary of peace. For now, take just a minute to simply focus in your heart, and continue to breathe deeply, and slowly. [1 Minute Pause]

The program begins with just a one minute pause with background music. For anyone beginning meditation, even spending just 60 seconds without jumping up into the intellect can be a challenge.

> We can think of life as a current of energy within us, a river of peaceful support that we all share. It connects us to each other, and sustains us. When you tap into your sanctuary of peace, within your heart, you can experience that current of energy, that river of life.

A few sentences of soothing words and imagery help to keep the listener relaxed and focused, and seed the notion of something enjoyable to be gained in the meditation.

> Take a little longer to sit quietly, breathe deeply and slowly, focus in your heart, and simply be attentive to the river of life within you. [2 Minute Pause]

> It's not often easy to quiet the mind, especially at the beginning. The mind is like a flywheel, with its own momentum, and takes a while to spin down. To think about relaxing the mind is to stimulate it further. So the best approach is to simply watch it, recognize when its spinning, and bring your focus back to your heart.

The paragraph above underscores for the listener that quieting the mind may not be easy, making it OK to find this process challenging at first. Then a bit of advice is offered—simply watch the mind, and refocus in the heart.

> Take a little longer to sit quietly, focus in your heart, and simply attend to the river of life within you, within your sanctuary of peace. When you find yourself thinking, refocus in your heart, and breathe. [4 Minute Pause]

> Most of the time we're busy; doing something, thinking about something we'll do, or thinking about something we did. In your sanctuary of peace, there is nothing to do. It's like sitting by a peaceful river on a Sunday afternoon, and simply watching the water. Soon the placid scene in front of you begins to reflect inside you, and you feel quiet calm, and still.

More soothing imagery, and a suggestion for becoming calm, like a placic river. We are so used to being overstimulated that mixing in these narrative interludes in the meditation helps to satisfy the mind's craving for content, while keeping the listener in a peaceful, inwared focus.

Take some more time to experiment by quietly focusing in your heart, and simply being, without the need to do anything. [5 Minute Pause]

We spend so much of our time being active, thinking, doing, influencing, creating. But your sanctuary of peace is a place for receiving. What you receive there can be described as comfort, healing, love, or peace. Receiving these doesn't require any action on your part, or any thought. All you need to do is just be open, relaxed, and receptive, and they will come.

We're programmed from an early age to be active, productive, to build things, get ahead, help others. We learn to prioritize doing over being, so simply being in a state of receptivity can be a challenge for us. Meditation offers us the opportunity to step back, listen within, and receive the meaning life has for us.

Take a little while to quietly focus in your heart, rest in your sanctuary of peace, relax, open and receive. [6 Minute Pause]

It's almost time for the end of the narrated portion of this experience. If you wish, get ready to bring yourself back to your physical surroundings, and come fully into your outside world. Or if you prefer, take a while longer to visit your sanctuary of peace, rest, and receive. [20 Minutes]

CHAPTER 3

YOUR RECORDING SETUP

When I first began making guided meditations, the only decent way to create a professional sounding program was to go into a fancy recording studio. That's still an option, but you can probably get away with paying less than I did back in the old days. Lucky you!

And today you've got some more interesting choices as well. There are a variety of decent, entry level microphones that can plug directly into your computer, or tablet. And there are also some inexpensive or free recording apps.

Let's look at your two main choices for recording—commercial studio or home studio—and then we'll go into more detail about what's available for you at home.

HIRING A STUDIO VRS. RECORDING AT HOME

When you book time in a commercial studio, you won't have to worry about equipment or recording techniques. A recording engineer will handle all that for you. You'll just show up, read your script, and pay the tab. The studio may even have some resources handy for background music or sound effects, although you'd be well advised to find your own ahead of time. (See Meditation Music & Background Sounds)

However, recording studios are all over the map in terms of the quality and experience they offer. They can vary from a rock musician's garage setup, to a multi-million dollar state of the art facility. Rates tend to correspond. A quick search for studios in your area should turn up quite a few options and give you some idea what you might expect to pay. Not everyone with a studio has much experience recording spoken word material, but if they have, that's a plus. You shouldn't have to book the most expensive studio in town to get the job done.

Hiring a Commercial Recording Studio: Pros & Cons

Pros:

- Professional recording equipment is already in place and ready for your project

- A recording engineer runs everything for you, and may offer some helpful guidance

- No need to learn software

- No equipment to purchase

Cons:

- Hourly rates to pay

- Level of professionalism, expertise, and personality of your service provider can vary

- Without a home studio setup you're always reliant on the outside studio

- You may need to try more than one place before finding one you like

If you decide hiring a commercial studio is the way to go, call around and try to actually speak to the person who will be helping you. Try to get a feel for the person who will be on the other end of the microphone from you, and decide whether you are comfortable with them. There should be plenty of studio options, so check around town until you find a setup you like.

Prior to your session, rehearse and prepare your narration. You might read your script to a friend, or practice with the voice memo app on your phone, to get some idea of how you're doing. (See Voicing Your Guided Meditation.) Book enough time so that you won't feel rushed. For a 20 minute program, allow at least 2 - 3 hours to run through your reading a few times, and get the editing and mixing done (background music, etc.) to your satisfaction.

Recording Your Program At Home: Pros & Cons

If you have patience, like learning new things, enjoy using your computer, want to take your time with your project, and prefer not to be concerned with studio rates, recording at home might be for you.

Pros:

- No hourly rates

- No time pressure – record at your leisure

- If you're planning on doing multiple guided meditations, investing in your own setup can easily pay for itself

- Ability to readily make adjustments to your program after you've had time to step back and review it, rather than having to go back to the commercial studio for more time

- Privacy — no recording engineer listening

- The joy of owning and learning to use recording gear

Cons:

- Cost of new microphone and other equipment adds up

- The learning curve for new software and the recording process may be a challenge

- No potentially helpful input from recording engineer

- It's all on you

SETTING UP YOUR HOME STUDIO

If you decide you'd like to try recording your program at home, here are three possible scenarios to consider, in order of increasing difficulty, expense, and sound quality. Take your time looking through the material below. If you find it interesting, home recording might be the right path to take. If it seems too involved or complicated, you would probably prefer recording in a commercial studio. There's no sense getting bogged down with the recording process when you really just want to make guided meditations, unless recording would be fun for you.

Home Recording Option #1: Cheap & Dirty

This is the approach to take if:

- You just want to make a guided meditation recording for your own use, to share with a friend, or to give to a counseling client

- You don't plan on duplicating, distributing, and/or marketing your program to the general public

- You don't care much about your sound quality, you just want to get it done

If that sounds like you, here's what you need to do:

1. Get an inexpensive microphone that you can plug directly into your phone, tablet, or computer. (See the list of Cheap & Dirty Mics below)

2. Prepare your script, and decide ahead of time exactly how long you want the pauses in your program to be.

3. Choose your background music or sound effects, and set those up on some kind of system to be playing in the background of your room.

4. Set up your mic so it's not more than 8 inches from your mouth.

5. Make your recording using the simplest voice memo app available on your phone or tablet.

6. Listen back to test out how well it meets your requirements.

7. Adjust your script/setup/delivery/pauses as needed, and repeat the operation until you are satisfied.

AGAIN, this is the dirty, lo-fi approach. Only do it this way if you don't care about sound quality, are not particular about your presentation, and don't plan to use your guided meditation in any sort of commercial application.

Cheap & Dirty Mics $0 - $260

Here are a few microphones to consider in order of quality, if you plan to take the Cheap & Dirty approach. (This is what's available as of this writing, and the list is by no means exhaustive. There are plenty of other choices out there.)

- First, least expensive ($0), and worst sounding: Use the microphone that's built into your computer, tablet, or phone. As far as quality is concerned, this is the worst possible choice. It's free, but it sounds like it.

- IK Multimedia iRig Mic Lavalier Microphone (about $50.) This is a "lavalier" or "lav" mic, which means it's a little one that clips onto your shirt, a few inches below your chin. Lav mics are normally used in video production because they are tiny and inconspicuous. I listed it here because it's cheap, and it will work OK for your purposes. Note that it has a mini-stereo audio jack. If your phone or tablet doesn't have a mini audio jack, well, you're out of luck with this one, unless you can find an adapter.

- Shure MV5 Digital Condenser Microphone (about $80). This cute little mic can plug into most any kind of computer, phone, or tablet. Comes with its own desktop stand, and has an optimization setting for voice.

- Audio-Technica AT2020USBi Cardioid Condenser USB Microphone (about $200). Audio-Technica is known for the quality of their gear, and this looks to be a decent USB mic. But check to make sure your equipment offers a USB connection. If not, you may be able to purchase an adapter that will work with this mic.

- Apogee MiC PLUS for iPad, iPhone, Mac and Windows (about $260.) This one is admittedly not so cheap, and also not so dirty. You'll get better sound with this than with either of the first two listed above. It comes with a mini-desktop stand, and for another $100 you could get a fancy boom-arm stand that attaches to your desk. You could also use this mic for Home Recording Approach #2, shown next.

Home Recording Option #2: Still Cheap But Not As Dirty

The main problem with Approach #1 above, is that you have no ability to edit and mix your audio. You're playing your background music in the background while you voice your script, and recording the whole thing at once. The background music won't sound very good, because it's all going through that little microphone. And you can't adjust the volume of the background music after you've recorded, because it's on the same track with your voice. All in all, this setup is far short of ideal.

So if you care about your sound quality, and want to have more flexibility, and have a little patience, here's a better idea. Instead of using the simple voice memo app on your phone, use a recording program that offers multitrack recording. This is what you need for Option #2:

- Microphone you can plug directly into your computer or tablet

- Free Recording Software (often referred to as a DAW or Digital Audio Workstation) like Garage Band, Protools First, or Audacity

- The built-in speakers in your device and/or available headphones

- Some patience to learn the recording software

(Tips on how to best go about making your recording at home are below.)

All-In-One Bundles You Can Buy $200 - $220

Here are a couple all-in-one packages that could offer a relatively easy entry-level home recording setup, including software. These include a mic and more, and while not offering the highest quality, they would be a big step up from Option #1.

- Focusrite Scarlett Solo Studio Recording Bundle (about $220). This bundle has just about everything you need to get started recording on your computer. It includes a mic, mic preamp/audio interface, cable, headphones and Protools First recording software. Get a mic stand and a pop filter and you'll be all set.

- PreSonus AudioBox 96 Studio USB 2.0 Hardware/Software Recording Kit. (about $200) This one is like the Scarlett Solo bundle, but offers the less popular Studio One Artist DAW Software instead of Protools First.

Notice that the above kits cost less than just the Apogee microphone I listed in Option #1 above. The reason for that is simple: The mics in those kits are not so great. If you want to get more particular about your sound quality, you will need to spend more.

Home Recording Approach #3: Not So Cheap, Best Sound Quality

Option #2 above is OK, but there are still a couple problems if you want a quality recording: The microphone still won't be quite up to pro standards, and your audio system for listening back to your recording won't be very good. So here's what you'll need to make your own *quality* recording at home:

- Computer or Tablet

- A Non-USB quality Microphone plus an Audio Interface/Mic Preamp

- Mic Stand

- Audio Recording and Editing Software

- Speakers and/or Quality Headphones that connect to your computer/tablet

- Patience to learn how to put that all together and work the software

If you'd like to get more particular about setting up your own studio at home, and can afford to spend more, here's what to look for. These components are the same kind included in the bundled deals in Option #2, but by picking and choosing each part (and paying more) you'll get better quality. If you'd rather keep it simple and lean toward a bundle like the ones listed above, you can skip this section.

Microphone & Audio Interface

Is the microphone the most important component in the recording process? No, your voice is! The microphone is the *second* most important component in the recording process. So, if you plan to record at home, it pays to invest in a good mic.

Great mics can cost thousands, but here are a few excellent professional voice mics to consider in the $300 - $400 range. There are many other choices in this range as well.

- Electro-Voice RE20 (about $400) The RE20 is a long time broadcast favorite mic. It's a mic that makes the voice stand out in a particular way that sounds good on the radio. If you have a very soft, unfocussed sounding voice, this one might help your voice be more easily understood.

- Shure SM7B (about $400) This is another longtime favorite dynamic mic for broadcast and spoken word recordings.

- AKG C214 (about $360) This mic is a bit of a bargain, because it's essentially the same as a much more expensive AKG 414 mic, but without some bells and whistles you don't need. It's a beautiful sounding mic on voice and a variety of instruments as well.

- Audio-Technica AT4040 (about $300) This one is in many ways similar to the AKG 214. I have not done a side by side comparison, but my guess is that if you would like the AKG for recording your speaking voice, you'd probably also like the AT4040.

You'll also need a mic stand, either one that stands on the floor, or clamps onto your desk. Not very expensive. Buy one where you get your mic.

And while you're at it you should get what's called a "pop filter." When you pronounce a "P" at the beginning of a word, there's a kind of low "whump" sound that mics make, called a "plosive." The pop filter helps cut down on that problem. Also not very expensive.

Microphone Preamp/Audio Interface

With any of the four mics listed above, and as with any non-USB microphone, you will need an audio interface/mic preamp that goes between the mic and your computer. If you are buying a condenser mic like the AT4040 or AKG C214, you will need an interface that supplies the mic with 48 volt power. Look for a switch that says "48V."

Audio interfaces typically offer between two and sixteen channels. But you won't need all those channels. You can get by with just two, or even just one channel.

Here are a few inexpensive audio interfaces that plug into your computer, available as of this writing. You can certainly spend a lot more, but these will do:

- Focusrite Scarlett 2i2 USB Audio Interface (about $160). Simple and straight forward.

- Mackie Big Knob Studio 3x2 Studio Monitor Controller (about

$220). More complicated. However, this one also can hook up to a pair of quality powered speakers. (See Speakers & Headphones, below.)

- Zoom U-24 Handy Audio Interface (about $110). Simpler than the Mackie, but still has all you need, including speaker hookups.

Before you buy, check to make sure any audio interface you're considering will plug into your computer or tablet, or that there is an adapter available.

Computer Software for Recording

You'll need an app in your computer or tablet for recording, editing, and mixing your guided meditation. For recording a guided meditation narration, and mixing it with your background music, you can get by with the free software that's widely available. But plan on spending time reading the manual, watching online tutorials, and experimenting until you're comfortable using this software. These programs are all similar, but all a little different. Once you've learned one, they all become easier to learn. But since you probably only need to learn one, that doesn't help you, does it? Learning to use your recording software is the most complicated part of recording at home. The rest is pretty simple.

Here are a three well-known free recording programs. All are free!

- Protools First. Protools is an industry standard for recording, editing, and mixing music and audio of any kind. Starting with the free version means that should you want to upgrade to any of the more professional versions of the program, you'll already be familiar with it.

- Garageband (for Mac only). Relatively easy to learn and fun, Garageband is really set up for music production, but will work fine for recording and producing guided meditations.

- Audacity. A more stripped down recording program than the two above, Audacity is popular with podcasters becuase it's simple and easy to use. It would be quite suitable for recording your guided meditation programs.

Speakers & Headphones

You will need to listen back to what you've recorded, and earbuds are not designed to give you the sound quality you need. Your computer speakers may be good enough to use, but not ideal. Good audio monitors will help you know what your program will sound like over a variety of listening options. And while a pair of quality headphones will work, it's best to also have a pair of speakers. The kind of speakers you'll want are "powered speakers," meaning they include their own amplifier.

The choices for speakers and headphones are legion. So many choices! Oy. Lean toward those that offer listening accuracy, versus hyped highs and bass, and get the best ones you can afford.

But how to plug your speakers into your computer? Most computers have a stereo mini-jack, and if yours does, you could get a "Y" adapter that lets you plug wires from both speakers into that little jack. That could work, but a better approach would be to use an interface like the Mackie Big Knob or the Zoom U-24 mentioned above. It will handle your microphone inputs, and your speaker outputs, and the speakers will get a cleaner sounding signal from the computer that way.

Where To Shop

Because buying gear like this can get a bit complicated, I suggest purchasing from an audio specialist retailer with a well-informed, patient sales team. Perhaps the best of these in the US is a company called Sweetwater, in Indiana. They love to help people with stuff like this. Sweetwater and other companies sometimes offer their own custom assembled bundles, with the best of each component for getting started, so check with them and see what they might suggest. Their bundles may be a step or two up in quality and expense from the two bundles I listed above.

MAKING YOUR RECORDING AT HOME
(If you're hiring a commercial studio instead of doing it yourself, you can skip this section.)

So let's say you've got a microphone, stand, pop filter, a mic preamp/ audio interface, headphones and/or speakers, and some computer software for recording. This is so exciting! Let's talk about what to do next.

Get A Room

It matters where you do your recording. For recording your speaking voice, non-echoey rooms are better than bright, bouncy sounding rooms. For your purposes, most rooms would be OK as long as we're not talking about tiled bathrooms, or big empty rooms with no furniture. Consider that vocal booths in recording studios tend to be fairly dead sounding, with absorbent materials on the walls, and few if any reflective surfaces. So in your home, a corner with carpet or rug on the floor, couches or a bed, and soft wall hangings would make an ideal spot for recording your voice.

Also, your room needs to be QUIET. No refrigerator noise, air conditioner, loud computer fan, traffic, TV, children, snoring husband, screaming girlfriend, or barking dogs should be tolerated. Turn off the phone.

Mic Placement

Plan to sit in a comfortable, supportive chair that doesn't squeak. Position your mic so it will be facing you, 6 – 8 inches in front of you, at an even height with your mouth. Make sure that the active side of the mic faces you—that's the side with the screen on it. If both sides have a screen, it's usually the side with the company logo, but check the manual or ask whomever sold you the mic to make sure. If your mic has a selectable pattern (cardioid, omni, figure 8, super-cardioid), select the cardioid pattern, which is the heart-shaped one.

Your pop filter will attach to your mic stand. Position the pop filter between the mic and your mouth. Does the pop filter material in front of your face look like nylon stockings? Try not to think about that.

Setting Levels

Once you have everything set up, you'll want to make a test recording to check that things are working, set your levels, and see if you're picking up any noise.

Set the microphone input knob on your audio interface to the half-way point. Using your recording software, select a single mono (not stereo) track to record on. Set the level of that track to "0," which is about 2/3 of the way up. Click the Record button. Sit in the hot seat and speak at the volume you'd normally be using to deliver your narration, which will hopefully be a fairly soft voice. (See Voicing Your Guided Meditation.) Read a few lines from your script, then stop speaking. Click Stop on your software.

The track you recorded on should now display a representation of your recorded content, that looks something like a jagged bumpy skyline with peaks and valleys. Ideally, the highest peaks should extend most of the way to the top and bottom edges of the track, but should not touch the top and bottom edges. If they touch or jam into the top and bottom, you'll probably also see a red mark on your record meters. That means you're recording is too hot, and hot in this case does not mean "attractive." Too hot means your sound will be distorted.

To make adjustments to your volume, don't change your voice or your mic position. Instead, adjust the input knob on your audio inter-face up or down as needed. Then try again, until your track shows your voice peaking almost to the top and bottom, but not going over. That's the sweet spot for you.

Next, think about noise. If you can hear noise in your room, it will be on your recording. Look at the places in your recorded track before, after, and between when you were speaking. Those places should be way down, with very little content showing between the peaks and valleys of your speaking voice. Some of what's there might be your breath, but other than that, it should be quite minimal. If not, you might be picking up your computer fan, air conditioner, or some other noise.

When in doubt, listen back to your recording in headphones at a normal listening volume, and notice whether you hear noise in the background. A little bit of noise will be covered up by your back-ground music. More than a little bit will interfere with the clarity of your recording. If that's the case, you'll need to find a way to isolate your recording setup or move it further away from the source of the noise.

Take One

Once your levels are set and your script is in hand, do a full take. A nice thing about your recording setup is that if you make a mistake while reading your script, you don't have to start over. You can easily edit the mistake later. So, if you happen to say, "And take another slow, deep berth," don't stop. Just continue and say the same line over until you get it right.

When you've finished reading the script all the way through, go back to your software. There you'll be able to listen back and edit out the mistakes, leaving just the good parts of your take. I suggest doing things this way, rather than bouncing back and forth between your computer and your microphone as you go. Your voice will have more continuity if you read it all the way through first, and then edit later.

Timing Your Pauses

Working in this way, you can also time your pauses when you edit, instead of timing them while you're recording. So if you want to pause 20 seconds while your listener imagines they're walking along a beautiful mountain stream, you can leave out the pause while you're recording, and go right on to your next sentence. It will be easy to insert the pause when you edit, and you'll be able to set the amount of time exactly as you want it.

Catch Your Breath

Breath sound is a natural part of speaking sound. But for some reason, some audiobook publishers delete every single breath sound from their programs. I don't think this is necessary with your guided meditation, unless there's something unusually distracting about the sound of your breathing. For the most part, you can leave in your breath sounds.

However, when you are editing your script, you'll need to be careful about the breath sounds between the words or sentences you are cutting together. A breath sound has a natural slope in and out. Don't chop into the middle of a breath sound, or it won't sound natural. Either include a whole breath sound, or leave it out entirely.

S, T, K

After you've been editing for a while, you may begin to notice that certain consonants, like S, T, and K, are visually identifiable in your audio tracks. For example, Ts are often the little blips at the beginning or end of a word. And here's a fun fact: All Ts sound pretty much exactly the same. That's because there is no "pitch" or musical note in a consonant, the way there is in your vowel sounds. As a result, if for some reason you happened to leave out an S or a T in one word, you can just copy it from another word and paste it in where you need it. Isn't that cool? No? Well, I think that's cool. Nevermind then.

Add Music & Fine Tune

Once you have recorded and edited your narration, and obtained your background music, it's time to mix.

Import your music file into your music recording software, and place it on a separate stereo track, according to the instructions in your software. (See Meditation Music & Background Sounds.)

Set the volume of your music well below the volume of your voice. Set your music level high enough that when you're listening to your voice at a comfortable level, the music can still be heard easily, but does not overpower or distract from your voice.

Test out your program by playing it back, before you do a final mix. That means you should listen to your guided meditation as if you were one of your listeners. Sit back with headphones, or turn on your good speakers, and do your meditation. As you listen, notice anything about the program that catches your attention, distracts you from the process, or could be better. This is your chance to make the important adjustments that can take your program from OK to excellent. Specifically, be aware of:

- Any pauses that don't seem long enough, or are too long. It's not unusual to find that your pauses are not long enough, once you have a chance to sit back and listen with your background music in place.

- The volume of background music relative to the narration

- Any words or phrases in your script that could be smoothed out or improved.

Mixing

Once you have made any corrections to your program and are satisfied with it, it's time to mix it down to a single stereo file. Here are some technicalities to familiarize yourself with.

A Bit Of Verb

"Reverb" is the natural sound of the reflections of any sound as it bounces off the surfaces of a room. This is not the same as "echo." Echo is the sound slapping against a wall in distinct and diminishing instances. Reverb is the smoother and more gentle tailing off of a sound.

Unless you have a particular reason in mind, you'll want to stay away from adding reverb to your narration. But I do use it on affirmations in my guided meditation recordings, or when the meditation includes some kind of quote from an angel, spiritual being, or departed soul. A little reverb makes that part of the program stand apart from the rest.

Your recording software (or "DAW") probably includes the ability to add reverb. Look for it under "Effects" in the Mixing Board panel. Experiment with different types of reverb offered, and different amounts. You usually don't need much. You'll find that a little goes a long way.

Compression & EQ

EQ or "equalization" adjusts the bass, treble, and midrange frequencies of your sound. Compression evens out the volume peaks. Using EQ and compression takes some practice, and a little training helps too. Your DAW will probably include the ability to add compression and EQ, but if you would like to learn more, do a bit of Youtube research. EQ and compression are more advanced recording techniques, and while they can be important, they're a bit beyond what we should be covering in this book.

Making Your Final File

If you're planning on delivering your program directly onto the internet or to your audience in any form other than a physical CD, you'll probably want to mix to an MP3 file. Follow the instructions in your recording app for mixing to a file, or "exporting your audio" as it also may be called.

You'll find that there are several different "bitrate" levels or resolutions possible for your MP3 file. Your selection will depend on how your program will be published, because different publishers and audio distributors have different requirements. Many of them ask you to upload MP3 files that are 192Kbps. A higher rate of 256Kbps is also commonly used, with 320Kbps being the highest bitrate possible for an MP3 file. You can always resave your file at a lower bitrate, but scaling up from a low bitrate to a higher one is not advisable. So if you're unsure, save at the highest bitrate possible.

Of course, you can save copies at various bitrates for different purposes. For example, if you have a high resolution copy, but you'd like to have a copy to email to friends, and don't want the file to be very big, save another copy at 192Kbps and use that for emailing. It will be much smaller in size than a higher resolution file.

If you plan on making duplicating CDs of your program, you will need to save it as a .WAV or .AIFF file, which are high resolution formats, instead of MP3. In any case, I would suggest saving your working file (the one from your editing software), so that if you need to make any changes down the line, you won't have to go back to square one. While you're at it, why not also save one mix file as a high resolution .WAV or .AIFF file, even if you're not making a CD. You can always resave that as an MP3 later.

And that's what you need to know about recording and mixing your file!

CHAPTER 4

VOICING YOUR PROGRAM

Once you have your script in hand, and have a commercial studio or home studio set up and ready to record, it's time to create the voice track for your guided meditation. I covered tips for delivering your narration in my book, *The Healing Waterfall, 100 Guided Imagery Scripts for Counselors, Healers & Clergy*. And since my advice from the earlier book still holds, I will plagiarize myself and reprint it here, adapted slightly to suite this printing.

Take Your Time

Speak at a fairly slow pace to help your listeners settle into a nice, deep relaxed state of mind. If you think you are speaking slowly, you can probably speak still slower and still not be speaking too slow!

Speak Softly

When recording you have the advantage of using a microphone that can easily pick up your softest voice. Speaking in a soft voice can establish a tone of intimacy that will help your listeners feel welcome, safe and relaxed. If you feel as though you must speak in a loud, booming "voice of authority," are you really sure you want to record a guided meditation?

Pause Between Thoughts

Give your listener time to absorb what you're saying. If you say, "Imagine you're walking along a forest path, early in the morning," create a pause to give them time to fill in the picture, feel their feelings, and hear the stream in the background, in their mind's ear. Then continue on to the next thought. A 20 second pause may seem like a lot to you when you're making your recording, but to the listener it can go by very quickly. (When making a recording, you can add pauses in and adjust the timing in the editing stage. More on this in the previous chapter, Your Recording Setup.)

As a general rule, pause a bit between sentences, and pause a bit longer between paragraphs. Adapt your delivery according to the content, but establish a reliable rhythm so your listener will know what to expect. That will help them relax further.

Beyond that, there are times when you'll want to give your listeners extra-long pauses. If you have asked your listener to do some deep processing, make your script include the words "Take some time with this," "I'll give you some time now," or something similar. Then give your listener a full minute or more before going on.

Read As If You Are Telling A Story

This is a tough one for many people, but I do encourage you to read as if you were telling a story. Put some expression into your voice. It's true that some people who do guided imagery deliver their material in a dull monotone, intending to thereby lull their subject into a deep trance. But that's not necessary, and it's dead boring! The idea here is not to put someone to sleep (unless it's a guided meditation for sleep), but to help them have a rich inner experience. Putting some color in your voice helps the listener go deeper into the story, and into their experience. As long as you speak softly, and read at a fairly slow, steady pace, your client will go inward just fine, even while you include some expression.

Your Attitude Is Key

Most importantly, your attitude toward your listener is crucial. If you are feeling patient, kind, and caring, it will come across in your voice, and your listener will feel it. It will help them feel safe and cared for. More than anything, your caring will allow them to relax, open up, heal and transform.

Simply put, love heals. I would encourage you to do whatever you need to do to get in touch with your own love before you deliver your narration. Your love will make the work much, much more effective.

CHAPTER 5

MEDITATION MUSIC & BACKGROUND SOUNDS

Most guided meditation programs include background music, generally of the ambient or "new age" genre. Your background music should help your listeners relax and drop down deeper, and not distract from your narration. Look for music with the following qualities:

- Slow tempo

- Even volume all the way through

- Any lead instruments or melodic lines should not be strident or distracting

- Sounds should be soft and soothing

- The music should be appealing and enjoyable enough that you would want to play it by itself in your home

In addition, the emotional sense of the music—the feelings it evokes—should fit with and help support your program. If the music sounds sad or poignant, it might be appropriate for a guided meditation in which you're trying to help the listener process grief. Consider whether that's the right tone for the subject of your meditation. Music that is especially etherial might be a good choice for a program with a metaphysical focus.

There is certainly no shortage of background music available. Search for "stock music," "music library," or "production music," and drill down the categories to find what you need. You should be able to find something suitable within any budget. You could even try the search results for "free meditation music." But be aware that just because it's called music, doesn't mean it's good music! Listen, and evaluate. I would suggest trying out a few different offerings with your narration, to see what seems to work best.

Music File Format

Whenever possible, get your music in a high resolution format. Common high res formats include .WAV, and .AIFF. MP3 files are not considered high resolution, and further, the resolution of MP3 files themselves varies quite a bit. The advantage of MP3 is that the file sizes are small so they upload and download quickly, and don't take up much storage space on provider's systems. But in decreasing file size they sacrifice sound quality.

That being said, because your background music will be mixed well below the level of your voice, a decent MP3 music file will probably be fine. Get a high resolution file to insure audio quality, but it's OK to use an MP3 if that's what you can get. It should also go without saying that you want a stereo music file, not mono. A stereo music file will make your recording sound much richer.

Other Background Sounds

There's certainly no rule that says you have to use music in the background of your guided meditation. Certain nature sounds can be very effective backgrounds, especially ocean waves, streams, or fountains. Water sounds are great as long as they are very gentle and peaceful. You can also try combining music with other background sounds.

I've used the sound of a train recorded from inside a sleeper car as the background to a sleep meditation. And I've heard a recording of a wooden sailboat used in some programs. A search for sound effects will bring you to various online resources that you can scan for anything you can imagine. As long as you own license to use the recording, and it works with the meditation you're creating, use whatever best suits your needs.

A Music Gift For My Readers

I've been making music for guided meditation as long as I've been making guided meditations, which is a long time! I've put together a Free Guided Meditation Music Album for you, which you can download at my website. Visit TheHealingWaterfall.com/readersgift and use the password *ireadmaxh2* to log in. You'll receive a coupon and a link to download your free music set, including four different music selections totalling over an hour. Enjoy!

CHAPTER 6

PUBLISHING &
DISTRIBUTING
YOUR PROGRAM

Perhaps you plan to use your guided meditation recording in your own work, with friends, or as part of an online course or other publication that you are already aligned with. In that case once your program is mixed down into the files you need, you'll be all set. But if you would like to see your work reach a wider audience, a number of possibilities are available.

Digital Distribution

There are many, many digital distribution channels online for audio programs, some of whose names are probably familiar to you, and many who may not be. A sampling of these include 7digital, 8tracks, Akazoo, Amazon Music, Anghami, AWA, eMusic, Google Music Store, and there are dozens more. The easiest way by far to reach all potential markets with the least amount of effort is to publish your program through an aggregation and distribution company like CDBaby. For a small fee, CDBaby will get your program into all the outlets. That also includes distributing your physical CD, if you have one, as well as your program in digital form.

CD Replication

If you would like to have physical CDs manufactured, there are many companies that can help you, and handle everything from your cover art, to a barcode, to shrink-wrapping the finished product. CDbaby offers those services as well. But two the two largest companies that do this are Discmakers.com and OasisCD.com. And surprise, all three companies are owned by the same people! There's virtually no difference between hiring any of them to do the job, and they will all serve you well.

However, if you are planning to make CDs, my personal recommendation is to make the smallest quantity you think you will possibly need. There's nothing quite like having boxes of CDs filling your garage, and going nowhere. I'm not saying I know that from personal experience, but, well I do. Not every project is a smash hit! Unless you have very well informed information on the number of CDs you'll be able to sell, think small.

Other Channels And Outlets

There are a number of online apps and websites that will publish your guided meditation, assuming it meets their approval. One of the most popular of these is called InsightTimer. InsightTimer won't pay you for your guided meditation streams, although it may bring you a bit of free publicity. As is typical with similar platforms, it seems that authors who were the earliest to publish with them receive the lion's share of attention.

Another way to see your guided meditation receive attention, and potentially generate revenue for you, is to publish it as part of a larger online course about any topic you may be an authority on. Insight-Timer also allows you to publish online courses, which they do pay royalties for. Other popular platforms for online courses include Udemy, and DailyOM. These are non-academic platforms, and are not associated with educational institutions, but are highly popular places for people to learn a variety of subjects, including those related to self-help, personal growth, and spirituality—things that guided meditation programs tend to fit in with nicely.

Youtube is a very popular place to publish your own guided meditation for free, and you can place a link to your own website on your Youtube video and channel. You can publish an audio program on Youtube as the sound track for any video, even if the "video" is a single still image.

And of course you can always publish your guided meditation on your own website, to stream online, or download, or both. Your web designer should be able to do that for you very quickly and easily. If you're already selling products from your website, adding a down-loadable audio file as a new product should be a simple matter.

Rights Ownership

Before you publish a guided meditation in any form, be sure that you have legal license for the material, including the script and the music. Any music you purchase should come with specific information about how you are legally allowed to reproduce and publish it. The same holds true for the script you are reading from, if you have not written it yourself. If you are not sure you are allowed to publish any material, get in touch with its author or creator. In most cases you'll be able to work out a licensing deal with them. (See Recording Your Guided Meditation, for more information about music and a link to music for free.)

CHAPTER 7

CONDUCTING LIVE GUIDED MEDITATION

Most of this book is about making a guided meditation recording to share with listeners at some point in the future. But if you are a counselor, yoga instructor, clergy, or teacher, perhaps you have the opportunity to do live guided meditation. That might mean reading from a script, or improvising something on the spur of the moment; and it might be for just one listener, or a bigger audience.

Live Feedback

The main difference in doing a live program is the feedback you can receive from your audience while your meditation is in progress. If you're leading a group, your natural intuition and sensitivity to the energy in the room can go a long way toward letting you know whether they are with you.

If you are doing counseling or therapy work of some kind, and leading just one person in a guided meditation, it's not against the rules to ask them for feedback during your process. The trick is to elicit the feedback you need without bringing them up out of the meditation. So, you'll want to give them a way to signal you with the minimum output possible.

For example, if you've told your listener to take their time with an inner process, you can watch them silently for a while, and then say something like, "and when you're ready to continue on, just quietly raise one finger on your right hand to let me know." You can use this same technique with a group.

If you see your listener or listeners begin to fidget, or move their facial muscles, you might say, "and if this is making you uncomfortable, just quietly raise one finger…" and so on.

I've done a good bit of guided imagery on the phone with clients, and in that situation I'll say, "and without coming up out of the meditation, if you're doing OK and are ready to continue, just say 'OK.'"

Improvisation

If you've experienced a lot of guided meditation yourself, or if you've used a number of scripts such as the ones in my books, perhaps it's time to begin conducting guided meditation on the fly. You can always use the tried and true format outlined here—beginning with deep breaths, a transition like a staircase, balloon, or other conveyance, followed by a visit to a peaceful setting. Then let any recent topic of conversation with your listeners influence where you go next.

Doing this is not unlike making up a bedtime story for a child. If for example, your six year old had something scary happen to them during the day, you might tell them a story about a brave little boy or girl who knew how to make scary things disappear, and focus on happy thoughts. You can apply the same principle to your guided meditation.

All of the techniques covered in the script examples can be used when you're making up a guided meditation on the fly. Here is a list of some of the things we've covered.

- Inductions and transition, both gradual and quick

- Breath focus

- Using high quality background music or nature sounds

- Use of sight, sound, touch, taste and smell

- Pauses of varying lengths of time

- Visualizing light, color, water

- Meeting with guides, angels, spiritual figures, and loved ones

- Theater of the mind

- Head-to-toe relaxation sequence

- Projecting into the future

- Hedging your bets to avoid having the listener fail

- Metaphors from nature

- Affirmations

- Humor

- Dramatization of a current situation to set up the listener for change

- Seeding the idea of taking steps out in the world

- Rehearsal for success

THANK YOU!

Thank you for taking the time to receive the information I've put together for you about one of my favorite things: Guided Meditation.

I hope you've found this material helpful and enjoyable.

Let all the benefits of this program stay with you. And whenever you're ready, open your eyes, and feel awake, alert, and refreshed!

100 MEDITATION SCRIPTS
THE HEALING WATERFALL
100 Guided Imagery Scripts For Counselors, Healers & Clergy

Whether you're a counselor, teacher, healer, or pastor, in this collection you'll find the perfect script for your listeners. Choose from 100 evocative guided inner journeys that soothe, inspire, and delight. 400 Pages. Topics include:

- Finding Peace and Calm
- Healing and the Mind-Body Connection
- Improving Sleep
- Emotional Wellbeing and Happiness
- Visualization for Success
- Learning to Meditate
- Higher Guidance and Insight
- Connecting with Spiritual Figures
- Kids and Family
- 12-Step Programs

Find it at TheHealingWaterfall.com, and wherever books are sold.